Combat Engineering Equipment of the Warsaw Pact

Combat Engineering Equipment of the Warsaw Pact

Russell Phillips

Shilka Publishing
www.shilka.co.uk

Copyright © 2017 by Russell Phillips.

All rights reserved. No part of this publication may be reproduced, distributed or transmitted in any form or by any means, including photocopying, recording, or other electronic or mechanical methods, without the prior written permission of the publisher, except in the case of brief quotations embodied in critical reviews and certain other noncommercial uses permitted by copyright law. For permission requests, write to the publisher, addressed "Attention: Permissions Coordinator," at the address below.

Shilka Publishing
Apt 2049
Chynoweth House
Trevissome Park
Truro
TR4 8UN
www.shilka.co.uk

Book Layout ©2017 BookDesignTemplates.com

Ordering Information:
Quantity sales. Special discounts are available on quantity purchases by corporations, associations, and others. For details, contact the "Special Sales Department" at the address above.

Combat Engineering Equipment of the Warsaw Pact/ Russell Phillips. —1st ed.
ISBN 978-0-9955133-4-1

Contents

Introduction 1
River Crossing 3
    Snorkelling 4
    Swimming 6
    Vehicle-Launched Bridges 7
    Pontoon Bridges 22
    Amphibians and Ferries 32
    Bridging Boats 37
    Line of Communication Bridges 45
Mine Warfare 53
    Minelaying 53
    Mine Detection 60
    Mine Clearance 64
Armoured Engineer Vehicles 75
Recovery and Repair Vehicles 83
Earth-Moving Equipment 103
Image Credits 113
Digital Reinforcements: Free Ebook 117
About Russell Phillips 119

Introduction

The Warsaw Pact (more formally, the "Treaty of Friendship, Co-operation, and Mutual Assistance") was formed on 14th May 1955. Officially, it was created in response to the formation of NATO in 1949, and the re-armament and integration of West Germany into NATO. Another, albeit unacknowledged, motive was a Soviet desire to control Eastern European military forces. The Warsaw Pact was disbanded at a meeting of defence and foreign ministers on 25th February 1991. The Soviet Union was dissolved the following December.

The signatories of the Warsaw Pact were:

Albania
Bulgaria
Czechoslovakia
German Democratic Republic (DDR)
Hungary
Poland
Romania
Soviet Union

In 1962, Albania supported China over the Soviet Union in the Sino-Soviet split. They severed relations with the Soviet Union and ended active participation in the Warsaw Pact. In 1968,

Albania protested the invasion of Czechoslovakia, and later that year, they formally withdrew from the treaty.

Warsaw Pact combat engineering equipment was simple, rugged, and supplied in larger quantities than in the West. Combat experience in Afghanistan and in the Middle East showed it to be effective. The conscription system used by Warsaw Pact armies meant that training time was limited. This in turn meant that individual engineers were trained on specific tasks, and were less flexible than their Western counterparts. This was offset to some extent by the quantity of equipment that was provided to them. Both peacetime exercises and experience in Afghanistan demonstrated that the Soviet army's engineers were an effective force. The non-Soviet Warsaw Pact armies were not tested in combat, save for the invasion of Czechoslovakia in 1968. Their engineers' training was based on the Soviet model, and their equipment was similar if not identical, although often not as modern. This suggests that they would have been similarly effective, although the older equipment may have had a negative impact.

Throughout this book, armour angles are given in degrees from the vertical: so 0° is vertical, and 90° is horizontal. Where the armour is at an angle, the effective armour thickness is listed in square brackets.

River Crossing

During the Cold War, the Soviet army studied the disposition of rivers in Western Europe. It concluded that they would have to cross water obstacles up to 100m wide every 35 to 60km. Every 100 to 150km, they would encounter a water obstacle between 100m and 300m wide. Every 250 to 300km, they would encounter one that was wider still. In a war in Western Europe, the Soviet army expected to advance an average of 100km per day, leading to a significant number of river crossings. NATO would obviously try to destroy bridges to slow the advance. Therefore, the Warsaw Pact armies put a great deal of emphasis on their ability to cross water obstacles quickly and efficiently. A range of equipment was created to bridge gaps or ferry vehicles over rivers. River reconnaissance systems were developed to quickly measure water depth and river width. Some of these were mounted on sleds that were towed behind boats or amphibious vehicles. Many light armoured vehicles could swim. Main battle tanks carried snorkels that allowed them to wade through water up to five metres deep.

Most river crossings would have been assault crossings from the march, at sites that were only lightly defended, if at all. Reconnaissance patrols, equipped with specialised equipment, would find suitable sites. These would be up to platoon size, and operated up to 50km ahead of the main body. When a crossing site had been selected, a forward detachment would secure the site. This detachment would be two to three hours ahead of the main body, and would avoid enemy contact. A typical forward detachment would consist of a motor rifle battalion with an attached tank company and artillery battalion. Amphibians, ferries, air defence, anti-tank, and chemical defence units would also be attached. Heliborne, or occasionally airborne, troops could also be used in this role.

If the crossing site was defended, the attack would be carried out with significant artillery and air support. River crossings got priority for air support, and were considered particularly vulnerable to enemy air attack. Air defence assets would be deployed close to the crossing site, and would cross the river as soon as feasible to extend their coverage.

The crossing itself would be carried out by APCs or IFVs swimming across the river, supported by tank and artillery fire from the near shore. A few tanks may have crossed in the first wave, but most would provide fire from the near bank and cross later. Artillery and anti-tank units would cross immediately after the infantry to provide support in holding the bridgehead. Tanks would cross using ferries, bridges, or by snorkelling.

SNORKELLING

The ability to wade, or snorkel, through water up to 5m deep was a standard feature in Soviet main battle tanks. It seems likely that ferries or bridges were the preferred method of crossing water obstacles. That said, a 1971 British army intelligence report stated that the Soviet army considered snorkelling "a practical operation of war". Every tank crew was fully trained in it. Training took place on purpose-built sites with good facilities. Emphasis was placed on ensuring the crew were confident in their ability to snorkel well and safely.

Training was split into two phases. The first phase, lasting up to two months, concentrated on preparing the crews to operate tanks under water. Training covered swimming, diving, and carrying out procedures underwater whilst wearing escape masks. There was a good deal of safety training, which helped with crew confidence and morale. Rescue operations were practised on simulators. Crews were not allowed to move onto the second phase until they had passed this first phase.

In the second phase of training, the crew put their skills to the test. A five-metre deep lake was used to practice driving underwater. Initially, drivers would drive 90m underwater, progressing to 150m as their skills improved. At least some sites also had facilities for blind driving, with the driver guided only by the tank's gyro compass. After passing this second phase of training, crews would join their units.

Sealing and preparing a tank for snorkelling could take as little as 15 minutes. Older tanks took longer, up to half an hour. This would be done in a concealed area 3 to 5km from the river. When the tanks got to within 1 to 2km of the river, snorkels would be fitted. Tanks crossed at slow speed, in a column formation, with a 30m gap between vehicles. Drivers would not change gear or stop while in the water. Once across, the tank would have to stop while the crew removed the waterproofing. Until this was done, the turret could not be traversed or the gun fired. If a tank stalled in the river, the crew would flood the vehicle, then escape through the hatches.

An alternative method of snorkelling used winches to pull unmanned tanks across. A pair of armoured recovery vehicles would set up on the far bank with a pulley block and anchoring unit. Up to three tanks could be pulled across the river simultaneously. Using this method, a 10-tank company could cross a 200m-wide river in 35 minutes, assuming the tanks had already been sealed. The crews would cross separately, either in amphibious vehicles such as APCs, or on boats.

Snorkelling was not to be carried out under fire, and in some cases the banks would make it impossible. The entry bank had to have a slope of less than 25°, the exit bank one of less than 15°, and the current no more than three metres per second. In winter, drifting ice could damage the snorkel. The river bottom had to be reasonably firm, and free of boulders and craters.

Swimming

Many lighter AFVs were amphibious, and could swim across water obstacles. All APCs from the BTR-50 onwards, and all IFVs, were fully amphibious. The BRDM series of reconnaissance vehicles, and even some self-propelled artillery and AA vehicles, could swim. Many were propelled in the water by their wheels or tracks, although some used water jets to achieve better performance in the water.

Water obstacles would only be crossed under fire as a last resort. In these cases, a great deal of artillery would be called upon to support the operation. If at all possible, helicopter troops would be landed on the far bank, and attack simultaneously with the crossing. Tanks would stay on the near bank to provide covering fire, while amphibious armoured vehicles swam across. Once a bridgehead was established, tanks and other vehicles

BTR-80 Swimming

would snorkel or be ferried across. These would then continue the advance, while engineers used pontoons to make a permanent bridge crossing.

VEHICLE-LAUNCHED BRIDGES

Soviet estimates found that two-thirds of the river obstacles they would encounter in Europe were less than 20m wide. This led to the development of vehicle-launched bridges capable of quickly crossing these narrow gaps. The Polish army developed a tracked bridge, which was pushed into place by a tank. Small numbers of a T-34-based bridging tank were delivered to the Soviet army in 1957. This was soon superseded by the MTU-54, sometimes referred to as the MTU or MTU-1.

MTU-54

In 1958, the MTU-54 was introduced, based on a T-54 chassis. This mounted a simple 12.3m bridge, carried horizontally. Unlike later vehicles, the bridge was not folded for transit. To launch, a chain-drive mechanism moved the bridge forward, before it was lowered into place. This method had the advantage of keeping the silhouette low during launch and recovery operations. The MTU-54 could bridge an 11m gap, and had a load capacity of 50 tonnes. Launch time was three to five minutes, and recovery could take place from either end of the bridge.

It was fitted with a DShKM machine gun for defence, mounted in the centre of the vehicle. This had to be removed before launching the bridge. Later vehicles were fitted with a deep-wading snorkel, NBC protection, and automatic fire-suppression system.

SPECIFICATIONS: MTU-54

Crew: 2
Weight: 34 tonnes (including bridge)
Length: 12.3m (including bridge)
Width: 3.27m (including bridge)
Height: 2.87m (including bridge)
Ground clearance: 0.43m
Maximum road speed: 48km/hour
Maximum road range: 400km
Gradient: 60%
Vertical obstacle: 0.8m
Armament: 1x12.7mm DShKM MG

MTU-54

Armour:
Hull glacis: 100mm @ 60° [Effective: 200mm]
Hull sides: 70mm
Hull top: 30mm
Hull rear: 60mm
Belly: 20mm

MT-34 (Czechoslovakia)

Introduced in 1960, the Czech MT-34 mounted a scissor bridge on a T-34-85 chassis, with a boxy superstructure holding the cable winches and hydraulic units. A contemporary of the Soviet MTU-54, the bridge was much shorter than the Soviet design when in transit, making it less cumbersome. It was much easier to spot when launching, however, since the bridge was raised to vertical before being unfolded into place. It had a bow mounting for a 7.62mm DTM machine gun, but the machine gun was not usually fitted. The system served with various Warsaw Pact armies, in addition to the Czech army.

Specifications: MT-34

Crew: 3
Weight: 32 tonnes (including bridge)
Length: 8.5m (including bridge)
Width: 3.2m (including bridge)
Height: 3.7m (including bridge)
Ground clearance: 0.4m
Maximum road speed: 55km/hour
Maximum road range: 300km
Gradient: 45%
Vertical obstacle: 0.73m

Armour:
Hull glacis: 45mm @ 60° [Effective: 90mm]
Hull sides (upper): 45mm @ 40° [Effective: 59mm]
Hull sides (lower): 45mm
Hull top: 18-22mm
Hull rear: 45mm @ 50° [Effective: 70mm]
Belly: 18-22mm

MTU-20

From 1967, the MTU-20, based on a T-55 chassis, became the primary Soviet tank-launched bridge. In order to allow a longer span length whilst maintaining a low launch silhouette, the ends of the bridge folded back on top when in transit. When launching the bridge, a stabiliser at the front was lowered. The ends of the bridge were then unfolded and the bridge rolled forward, before being lowered into place. The MTU-20 had a

MTU-20

span length of 20m, with a load capacity of 60 tonnes. Launching the bridge took five minutes, recovery from either end took between five and seven minutes. Both launching and recovery could be carried out while the crew remained inside the vehicle. It was fitted with a deep-wading snorkel, NBC protection, and an automatic fire-suppression system.

SPECIFICATIONS: MTU-20

Crew: 2
Weight: 37 tonnes (including bridge)
Length: 11.64m (including bridge)
Width: 3.3m (including bridge)
Height: 3.4m (including bridge)
Ground clearance: 0.43m
Maximum road speed: 50km/hour
Maximum road range: 500km

Gradient: 40%
Vertical obstacle: 0.8m

ARMOUR:
Hull glacis: 100mm @ 60° [Effective: 200mm]
Hull sides: 70mm @ 40° [Effective: 91mm]
Hull top: 30mm
Hull rear: 60mm
Belly: 20mm

BLG-60 (POLAND/DDR)

The non-Soviet Warsaw Pact armies showed a preference for the more common scissor bridge design. Poland and East Germany jointly developed the BLG-60, which mounted a 50-tonne, 21.6m scissor bridge on a T-55 chassis. The bridge was launched by being lifted up to the vertical, then unfolded and simultaneously lowered over the gap. This design gave a quicker launch time than the Soviet designs, at the expense of a very high silhouette during launch. The BLG-60 was fitted with NBC protection and a deep-wading snorkel. An improved version, the BLG-67, was introduced in the late 1970s.

SPECIFICATIONS: BLG-60

Crew: 2-3
Weight: 37 tonnes (including bridge)
Length: 10.57m (including bridge)
Width: 3.48m (including bridge)
Height: 3.4m (including bridge)
Ground clearance: 0.43m
Maximum road speed: 50km/hour
Maximum road range: 500km

Gradient: 58%
Vertical obstacle: 0.8m

Armour:
Hull glacis: 100mm @ 60° [Effective: 200mm]
Hull sides: 7mm @ 40° [Effective: 9mm]
Hull top: 30mm
Hull rear: 60mm
Belly: 20mm

Bridge:
Weight: 6 tonnes
Length extended: 21.6m
Width: 3.2m
Load capacity: 50 tonnes

MT-55A (Czechoslovakia)

Like the earlier MT-34, the MT-55A mounted a scissor bridge, but was based on a T-55 chassis. A front spade stopped the vehicle being tipped over by the weight of the bridge. Launch time was two to three minutes, recovery time five to six minutes. Both tasks could be carried out from inside the vehicle. It could span an obstacle of up to 18m, and load capacity was 50 tonnes. A gap-measuring device and inclinometer were fitted, to help with finding a suitable site for the bridge. Other equipment included infra-red night-vision equipment, a snorkel, an automatic fire extinguisher, and NBC protection. Unusually, the Soviet army adopted the MT-55A, albeit in small numbers.

Initially, the scissor bridge carried by the MT-55A had circular holes in the sides of the bridge. Later models had solid sides. Multiple bridges could be combined to span larger gaps.

MT-55A (later model bridge)

SPECIFICATIONS: MT-55A

Crew: 2
Weight: 36 tonnes (including bridge)
Length: 10.05m (including bridge)
Width: 3.3m (including bridge)
Height: 3.5m (including bridge)
Ground clearance: 0.43m
Maximum road speed: 35km/hour
Maximum road range: 500km
Gradient: 30%
Vertical obstacle: 0.7m

ARMOUR:
Hull glacis: 100mm @ 60° [Effective: 200mm]
Hull sides: 70mm

Hull top: 30mm
Hull rear: 60mm
Belly: 20mm

BRIDGE:
Weight: 6.5 tonnes
Length extended: 18m
Length folded: 9.6m
Width: 3.3m
Track width: 1.15m (each)
Load capacity: 50 tonnes

MTU-72

In 1974, a new bridge layer entered service: the MTU-72. These were made from existing T-72 tanks with the turret removed, and a bridge-launching mechanism fitted instead. The bridge was of cantilever design, similar to that on the MTU-20, but made of an aluminium alloy. The 20m bridge had a load capacity of 50 tonnes and could span a gap of up to 18m. A second bridge could be launched from the first one to span a gap of up to 35m. Launching the bridge took three minutes, recovery eight minutes. Both launching and recovery could be carried out while the crew remained inside the vehicle.

A blade was fitted to the front of the hull. Primarily intended for stabilising the vehicle during launching and recovery, it could also be used as a bulldozer blade. A light machine gun, deep wading-snorkel, NBC protection system, fire-suppression system, and thermal smoke generation unit were also fitted.

MTU-72

SPECIFICATIONS: MTU-72

Crew: 2
Weight: 40 tonnes (including bridge)
Length: 11.64m (including bridge)
Width: 3.46m (including bridge)
Height: 3.38m (including bridge)
Ground clearance: 0.49m
Maximum road speed: 60km/hour
Maximum road range: 500km
Gradient: 60%
Vertical obstacle: 0.85m
Armament: 1x 7.62mm PKMS MG

BRIDGE:
Weight: 6.4 tonnes
Length extended: 20m
Length folded: 9.42m
Width: 3.3m
Load capacity: 50 tonnes

KMM

The Warsaw Pact made use of unarmoured bridge layers, based on lorries, as well as armoured variants based on tank chassis. The first of these was the KMM lorry-mounted bridge, which had a 12-tonne load capacity. A full system comprised five sections, each mounted on a ZIL-157 6x6 2.5-tonne chassis. Each lorry carried a single straight 7m bridge span. Four spans had integral trestle legs; the fifth span, which would connect to the far bank, had no legs.

To launch, the trackway was spread to its full width and the trestle legs were adjusted to ensure that the bridge would be level once placed. The vehicle reversed to the gap, and the bridge was raised to the vertical, before being lowered down into the final position. Further vehicles repeated the process, adding spans until the gap was completely bridged. A single span could be launched in about 15 minutes, and bridge a 9.5m gap. A full five spans took 45 to 60 minutes, and would bridge 34m. Recovery could take place from either end, in roughly the same time as it took to launch.

Specifications: KMM

Crew: 1+2
Weight: 8.8 tonnes (including bridge)
Length: 8.3m (including bridge)
Width: 3.15m (including bridge)
Height: 3.36m (including bridge)
Ground clearance: 0.31m
Maximum road speed: 40km/hour
Maximum road range: 430km
Gradient: 28%

Bridge:
Weight: 1,420kg
Length: 7m
Width: 3.95m
Load capacity: 15 tonnes

TMM

The KMM was replaced by the much improved TMM system, which entered service in 1964. A full set consisted of four 10.5m scissor spans carried on modified KrAZ-214 6x6 7-tonne lorries. Three spans had trestle legs with adjustments to allow for different depths. The fourth span had no legs, since it connected to the far bank. A later version, the TMM-3, used KrAZ-255B 6x6 7.5-tonne lorries, and featured improvements in the bridge-laying mechanism. The two versions could be readily identified by the position of the spare tyre. It was to the rear of the cab on the TMM, and on top of the cab on the TMM-3.

Before launching, the trestle legs were adjusted to the correct height and the trackways spread to their full width. The lorry reversed to the launch position, and a hydraulic girder raised the

TMM-3

folded span to the vertical. A cable and winch system straightened the span, and then lowered it into place. The trestle legs dropped into place as the span was lowered. Once in position, the cables were removed, the launching girder returned to the transit position, and the lorry drove away.

The standard four units could cross a 40m obstacle, although extra units could be added to bridge wider gaps. The bridge had a load capacity of 60 tonnes. An average crew would take 45 to 60 minutes to lay a four-section bridge. Recovery took the same time, and could be performed from either end.

In each division, some TMMs would be kept in reserve, and used to replace tank-launched bridges. The armoured bridge-layers would then re-join the advance unit.

The time to launch both **KMM** and **TMM** bridges could be halved with a well-trained crew. Both types could be laid underwater to reduce the possibility of detection. The difficulty of laying an underwater bridge increased the time taken by about 50%.

Specifications: TMM

Crew: 1+2
Weight: 19.5 tonnes (including bridge)
Length: 9.3m (including bridge)
Width: 3.2m (including bridge)
Height: 3.15m (including bridge)
Ground clearance: 0.36m
Maximum road speed: 55km/hour
Maximum road range: 530km

Bridge:
Weight: 7 tonnes
Length: 10.5m
Width: 3.8m
Load capacity: 60 tonnes

AM-50 (Czechoslovakia)

Czechoslovakia developed their own lorry-mounted scissors bridge, mounted on the rear of a Tatra 813 8x8 lorry. Launched in a similar manner to the Soviet TMM, the trestles on the AM-50 were adjusted hydraulically rather than manually. The bridge had a full width roadway, 4m wide and 13.5m long, with 50 tonne load capacity.

SMT-1 (Poland)

The SMT-1 was a lorry-mounted bridge developed in Poland. Organised in units of four, each vehicle carried a straight 11m span on a Star 660 6x6 2.5-tonne lorry. Unlike the Soviet vehicles, the bridge was launched over the front of the cab, rather than over the rear. The trackways were of a lightweight design

SMT-1 laying a multi-span bridge

and fixed, so that they did not need to be spread before launching.

Placing a span took three to five minutes, and was controlled from inside the cab. SMT spans were sometimes used as single-span bridges or as ramps onto pontoon bridges. Extra spans could be carried on a single-axle trailer.

SPECIFICATIONS: SMT-1

Crew: 1+2
Weight: 9.6 tonnes (including bridge)
Length: 11.97m (including bridge)
Width: 3.3m (including bridge)
Height: 3.15m (including bridge)
Ground clearance: 0.27m
Maximum road speed: 50km/hour
Maximum road range: 500km

BRIDGE:
Weight: 2.3 tonnes
Length: 11m
Width: 3m
Load capacity: 40 tonnes

Pontoon Bridges

LPP

The LPP light pontoon bridge was developed as a replacement for the Second World War-era DLP pontoon bridge. A full set consisted of 24 bow sections and 12 centre sections, each one carried on a GAZ-63 4x4 2-tonne lorry.

Pontoons were launched by gravity. Each pontoon had a turntable on top, holding the track and superstructure. Once in the water, the turntable was turned through ninety degrees and the superstructure assembled. Depending on the load to be carried, pontoon sections could be joined together or used singly.

An LPP bridge could be configured to carry loads of 12, 24, or 40 tonnes. The capacity was determined by the configuration of

LPP pontoon

pontoon elements. For a 12-tonne bridge, each support was a single pontoon. For a 24-tonne bridge, two pontoons were used for each support. Three pontoons per support would be required for a 40-tonne load. Assembly time was 50 to 60 minutes. LPP pontoons could also be configured as 24-tonne or 40-tonne-capacity ferries.

TMP

The TMP heavy pontoon bridge entered service in the Second World War, but only went into volume production after the war. It was the standard Soviet heavy pontoon bridge until it was replaced by the TPP. The pontoons were carried on ZIL-151 6x6 2.5-tonne lorries, which would back into the water, launching the pontoons by gravity. In the water, the pontoons were joined together. A complete set had 36 bow and 36 centre sections.

A full TMP set could create a 109m-long 70-tonne bridge, a 228m-long 50-tonne bridge, or a 518m-long 16-tonne bridge. Alternatively, TMP pontoons could be configured as 16-tonne, 30-tonne, or 50-tonne rafts, which would be powered by outboard motors or pushed by bridging boats.

TPP

The TPP was the heavy counterpart to the LPP, also developed as a replacement for a Second World War-era pontoon bridge, in this case the TMP. Like the LPP, each pontoon had a turntable holding the track and superstructure, which was turned through ninety degrees once launched. This allowed a TPP bridge to be constructed much more quickly than the older TMP.

A complete TPP set included 48 bow and 48 centre pontoons, eight trestles, four flotation drums, and twelve BMK-150 boats. In Soviet service, these were carried on 116 ZIL-151 or ZIL-157 6x6 2.5-tonne lorries. Other Warsaw Pact countries used locally-built lorries as transport vehicles.

A full TPP set could create a 205m-long 70-tonne bridge, a 265m-long 50-tonne bridge, or a 335m-long 16-tonne bridge. A working party of 384 men would take between two and three hours to build the bridge. Alternatively, TPP pontoons could be configured as 50-tonne ferries.

PMP

Introduced in 1962, the PMP marked a significant improvement in folding bridge design. The design concepts were adopted and further improved upon by the US army, resulting in the Ribbon Bridge. Each pontoon was made up of four sections,

PMP pontoon

folded in an accordion style when in transit, and with an integrated roadway. Initially carried on KrAZ-214 6x6 7-tonne lorries, they were later carried on more powerful KrAZ-255B 6x6 7.5-tonne lorries. In Czech service, they were carried on Tatra 813 8x8 8-tonne lorries, some of which were fitted with bulldozer blades to help with preparing river banks.

To launch a pontoon, the travel locks were released. The lorry then reversed up to the river bank, and braked sharply. Momentum carried the pontoon over a series of rollers, off the back of the lorry, and on into the river. The pontoon started to unfold automatically. It was fully unfolded, and a set of six locking devices used to make it fully rigid. The pontoons were connected together at the near shore, then swung into position. To recover a pontoon, the lorry reversed to the edge of the river. A winch and jib built into the lorry would be set up, and used to winch the pontoon back onto the lorry bed. The winch simultaneously re-folded the pontoon as it pulled it out of the water and onto the lorry. The pontoon was secured, and the lorry driven away. A full bridge took 50 minutes to assemble, while ferries took 8 to 20 minutes to assemble, depending on size. If the river was too shallow at the edges to accommodate the pontoons, TMM bridges could be used to connect the PMP bridge to the shore.

A standard PMP bridge was 227m long, with a load capacity of 60 tonnes, but the design was very flexible and offered other options. Extra hinges allowed the pontoons to be split lengthways. By doing this, and including full-size pontoons at regular intervals, a 389m, 20-tonne bridge could be built. Pontoons could also be used to create ferries of various sizes, with loads from 20 tonnes to 170 tonnes. A complete PMP pontoon set consisted of 32 river pontoons, four shore pontoons, and 12 bridging boats (BMK-T, BMK-130, BMK-130M, BMK-150, or BMK-150M).

PVD-20

The PVD-20 was an air-portable pontoon bridge designed for use by airborne forces. It could be dropped by parachute or carried by helicopter. A full set was made up of ten units. Each unit included two NDL-20 boats and trackways, made of duralumin to save weight. They were carried in ten GAZ-63 4x4 2-tonne or six ZIL-157 6x6 2.5-tonne lorries.

The PVD-20 could be used to build an 88m-long, 6-tonne bridge, or a 64m-long, 8-tonne bridge, in 50 minutes. Alternatively, ten 4-tonne rafts could be built in 15 minutes, six 6-tonne rafts in 20 minutes, or four 8-tonne rafts in 25 minutes.

Any of these configurations were sufficient to support the 3.4-tonne ASU-57 air-portable tank destroyer.

TZI

The TZI was a pontoon footbridge, first used during the Second World War. It consisted of floats made of rubberised fabric, filled with straw or hay, and with wooden boards and metal posts. The TZI was primarily used as a single-lane footbridge, but it could be built as a double-lane bridge to allow crew-served weapons to cross. A full set could be carried in a pair of light lorries.

A single-lane bridge was 56m long and could be constructed in 10 to 18 minutes. A double-lane bridge could cross a 28m obstacle, and took 14 to 22 minutes to construct. Sets of four or seven floats could also be combined into rafts, taking four or ten minutes respectively.

PPS

The PPS was a heavy girder pontoon bridge, with each pontoon built up from four sections (one bow, two central, one stern). The stern section included a power unit. Each section was carried on a ZIL-151 6x6 2.5-tonne lorry. An assembled pontoon was 23m long, and supported a 6m-wide full-width roadway. The maximum capacity of the bridge was 60 tonnes.

DPP-40

The DPP-40 was an air-portable pontoon bridge designed for use by airborne forces. As such, it was designed to be dropped by parachute. Development started in the late 1950s, and it was in service by the early 1970s. A full set consisted of 32 pontoons, each carried on a GAZ-66 4x4 2-tonne lorry, with 16 outboard motors and an extra GAZ-66 to carry auxiliary equipment.

Each pontoon consisted of a sealed metal box in the centre, with a pair of inflatable sides. In transit, the inflatable sections were folded on top of the centre piece. To launch, the vehicle reversed to the water's edge, then used a winch to unfold the sides and an air pump to inflate them. The assembled pontoon was then dropped into the water. If required, the sides could be inflated on the water, using a hose connected to the vehicle. Pontoons are connected together in such a way that the centre pieces form the roadway for the bridge.

A full DPP-40 bridge was 128m long, with a capacity of 40 tonnes. Alternatively, the pontoons could be formed into eight 40-tonne or sixteen 20-tonne ferries. When used as ferries, the outboard motors provided propulsion. Any of these configurations were able to support a BMD airborne fighting vehicle or ASU-85 air-portable tank destroyer.

LPB (DDR)

The LPB was a light pontoon bridge introduced in the 1950s, based on the Soviet Second World War DLP design. The pontoons had sheet steel hulls instead of the original's plywood, which improved stability and durability. A full set included 40 bow and 20 centre pontoons.

A set could bridge a 162m gap with a 10-tonne bridge, a 109m gap with a 16-tonne bridge, or a 58m gap with a 30-tonne bridge. Rafts with carrying capacities of 6, 10, or 30 tonnes could be created from the components, or pontoons could be assembled into assault boats.

PP-64 pontoon

PP-64 (POLAND)

The Polish PP-64 was inspired by the Soviet PMP folding pontoon bridge. Design work started in 1964, with the first production units delivered in 1966. Although inspired by the PMP, it was by no means a copy. The PP-64 had a different design which allowed for faster construction, but a lower load capacity for the standard bridge (40 tonnes compared to the PMP's 60 tonnes). A full PP-64 set included 48 river pontoons, six shore pontoons, twelve ramps, and six KH-200 bridging boats. A special connecting piece to join a PP-64 to a Soviet PMP was also included as standard.

A PP-64 set could bridge a 186m gap with a 40-tonne bridge, or a 97m gap with an 80 tonne bridge. On faster-flowing rivers, a second type of 40-tonne bridge configuration could be used to span up to 145m. In transit, pontoons were folded lengthways in an inverted V shape. To launch, the lorry (a Star 660 6x6 2.5-tonne) reversed up to the river edge. The pontoon was unfolded on the lorry, then launched into the water.

As well as bridges, PP-64 pontoons could be used to create a set of six ferries, each 14.8m long and 12.8m wide, with a 40-tonne load capacity. Alternatively, two large ferries could be constructed, each 37m long and 12.5m wide.

LMS (Czechoslovakia)

The LMS was a Czech light pontoon bridge, made out of aluminium. The bow pontoon was open, while the centre pontoon was fully enclosed. Once in the water the pontoons were assembled and bolted together, and then the trackway was added. The trackway could be full width, or more commonly, a dual-track type.

The bridge had a load capacity of 20 tonnes, and could be assembled in 40 minutes. The LMS could also be built as 10-tonne, 15-tonne, 20-tonne or 24-tonne rafts. Rafts were propelled in the water by an outboard motor, up to a maximum speed of 11km/hour. A complete set included 48 bow and 24 centre sections, carried on Praga V3S 6x6 3-tonne lorries.

SMS (Czechoslovakia)

The SMS was another Czech design, similar to the LMS, but larger and heavier. Classified by the Czech army as a medium pontoon bridge, it would be considered a heavy bridge by the US army. Built of steel, each full pontoon consisted of a single centre and two bow sections. Each pontoon was carried on a Praga V3S

6x6 3-tonne lorry. Decking and balking for three pontoons were carried on a single Tatra 111 6x6 10-tonne lorry.

Each bow pontoon had a winch and a removable deck, which were often not fitted. The centre pontoon had a fixed deck. Unlike other designs, pontoons had to be removed from their transport vehicles by crane, leading to a long construction time. A complete set included 72 bow and 36 centre sections.

SMS pontoon bridges could be built in 20-tonne, 40-tonne, or 60-tonne configurations. All took around 200 minutes to construct. Alternatively, the pontoons could be used to create rafts with capacities of 20, 40, or 60 tonnes. These were significantly quicker to construct, taking only 30 to 40 minutes.

PR-60 (Romania)

The PR-60 was developed as a replacement for the Soviet Second World War-era TMP, and could be used as a raft as well as a bridge. It did not use a folding design like the PMP, leading to a significantly longer construction time. Pontoons were carried on Bucegi SR-114 4x4 4-tonne lorries, and launched by gravity. Each lorry could carry two river pontoons, one on top of the other, or a single shore pontoon. The lorry had no recovery capacity, and so pontoons were recovered by crane. A complete PR-60 set had 56 river pontoons and four shore pontoons. A full set could make a 143m, 40-tonne bridge or an 80m, 60-tonne bridge.

Amphibians and Ferries

K-61

The K-61 tracked amphibious ferry was introduced in 1950, a direct result of wartime experience with American DUKW amphibious lorries supplied through the lend-lease program. It remained in Soviet service until the late 1960s. It was fully tracked, and based on a light AFV chassis, but was not armoured. The K-61 could carry eight wounded on stretchers or 40 fully armed infantry. Alternatively, it could carry up to five tonnes of equipment, a single lorry of up to 2.5 tonnes, or an artillery piece.

K-61

Loading was via ramps at the rear. Vehicles could be driven on, and a winch was provided for loading heavy equipment such as artillery pieces. It was driven through the water by a pair of propellers, at a speed of up to 10km/hour.

GSP

The GSP heavy amphibious ferry was introduced in 1959. A single ferry was made up of two distinct units, one left and one right. The two units were mirror images of each other, and not interchangeable. Before entering the water, a trim vane was erected at the front of the hull. The two units then entered the water separately and joined up in the water. Once linked, the pontoons, which were inverted while in transit, were swung upright, and the trackways deployed. It was important that the pontoons were both unfolded together, to avoid overbalancing the whole. Assembly time was 6 to 10 minutes.

The ferry had hydraulically operated ramps at each end, allowing vehicles to be driven on at one end and off at the other. Load capacity was 52 tonnes, enough to carry a main battle tank. It was reported that in good conditions, a tank could fire its main armament whilst on the ferry.

The vehicle itself was tracked, with a suspension similar to the PT-76 light tank. It had infra-red driving lights, although these were only used on land. The hull and pontoon were lightweight steel filled with plastic foam. The foam increased buoyancy and reduced vulnerability to enemy fire, allowing buoyancy to be retained even if the hull was holed. Propulsion in the water was provided by four propellers (two per vehicle), mounted in tunnels under the hull. Maximum speed in the water was 8km/hour.

SPECIFICATIONS: GSP VEHICLE UNIT

Crew: 3
Weight: 17 tonnes
Length: 12m
Width: 3.24m

GSP vehicle unit (left)

Height: 3.2m
Ground clearance: 0.35m
Maximum road speed: 40km/hour
Maximum road range: 300km
Gradient: 45%
Vertical obstacle: 0.8m

SPECIFICATIONS: GSP FULL FERRY

Weight: 34 tonnes
Length: 12m
Width: 12.63m
Draught (unloaded): 0.97m
Draught (loaded): 1.5m
Maximum water speed (unloaded): 10.8km/hour
Maximum water speed (loaded): 7.7km/hour
Load capacity: 52 tonnes

PTS

The PTS was introduced in 1966, as a replacement for the K-61. Larger than its predecessor, with a more powerful engine, it could carry up to 5 tonnes on land and 15 tonnes on water. Alternatively, it could carry up to 70 seated troops or 12 stretcher cases. The cargo area was open, but a tarpaulin was provided for protection from the elements.

PTS-M

The crew were seated in a cab at the front, and provided with full NBC protection. The engine was under the cargo compartment, and the vehicle was propelled in the water by two propellers in tunnels. A pair of rudders at the rear of the hull were used to steer. Before entering the water, the bilge pumps were switched on, and a trim vane erected at the front.

A boat-shaped trailer, designated PKP, was developed for use with the PTS. This had two small pontoons that folded onto the top when travelling, and were rotated through 180° and locked into place before entering the water. The trailer could be towed at speeds of up to 30km/hour when not loaded, down to 25km/hour when loaded. The trailer was not a success, as it was found to be unusable in anything other than very calm waters.

Rear ramps were used to load cargo, with a winch for loading heavy non-motorised loads. An infra-red searchlight and infra-red driving lights were fitted. A later version, with several minor improvements, was designated PTS-M.

PMM-2

Initially known to NATO as the ABS(T), the PMM-2 was introduced in 1974 as a replacement for the GSP ferry, and possibly the PMP pontoon bridge. It was based on a BAZ-5937 chassis, with two aluminium folded pontoons mounted on top, with entrance ramps. As the vehicle entered the water, the pontoons were hydraulically unfolded to either side. The vehicle itself formed a centre section. It was propelled in the water by water jets.

As a ferry, units could be used individually (40 tonne capacity), in pairs (80 tonne capacity), or in threes (120 tonne capacity). A single vehicle could be used as a bridge, to span gaps of up to 17m. Up to ten vehicles could be combined to span larger gaps, with no need for bridging boats.

PTS-2

The PTS-2, introduced in 1985, was an improved and modernised version of the PTS-M. It had a new suspension,

PTS-2

derived from the MT-T artillery tractor. The cab was larger than that on the older vehicle, and had NBC protection. The cargo space was larger, and it could carry up to 12 tonnes of cargo. As with the PTS-M, it had a pair of propellers for propulsion on the water, although a new engine meant that it was faster on both land and water.

BRIDGING BOATS

Soviet bridging boats were designed to be resilient to damage. They used compartments to limit flooding, and could stay afloat even if one or two compartments were holed and took on water. All designs were fitted with bilge pumps to remove any water taken on. The bilge pumps would be switched on prior to entering the water.

BMK-70 AND BMK-90

The steel-hulled BMK-70 dated from the Second World War, where it saw extensive service. It was normally carried on a trailer and towed behind a lorry.

The BMK-90 was developed in the 1950s as a replacement for the BMK-70. It had a corrugated steel hull, with a more powerful engine. Two wheels simplified launching and recovery of the boat, and could be removed or folded up alongside the hull when in the water. The later BMK-90M used duralumin instead of steel, and had a redesigned propeller shaft.

Specifications: BMK-70

Crew: 2
Weight: 2,450kg (without fuel)
Length: 7.83m
Beam: 2.1m
Depth: 1.5m
Draught: 0.64m
Maximum speed: 20.5km/hour (unloaded)
Towing power (forward): 681kg

Specifications: BMK-90 (BMK-90M in brackets)

Crew: 2
Weight: 2,450kg (without fuel)
Length: 7.83m
Beam: 2.1m
Depth: 1.5m
Draught: 0.53m (0.52m)
Maximum speed: 20.5km/hour (unloaded)
Maximum speed: 8km/hour (loaded)

Endurance: 14 hours
Towing power (forward): 1,100kg
Towing power (reverse): 1,400kg

BMK-130

Developed for use with the PMP pontoon bridge, the BMK-130 also gradually replaced the BMK-90. It was usually towed by a ZIL-131 6x6 3.5-tonne or ZIL-157 6x6 2.5-tonne lorry. A pair of integrated wheels negated the need for a separate trailer. These wheels were swung forward to the side of the hull when in the water. The boat had a steel hull and a single propeller driven by a two-stroke, 100hp diesel engine. It could achieve speeds of up to 19km/hour in the water.

As well as its use with pontoon bridges and for river reconnaissance, the BMK-130 was used to carry infantry reconnaissance teams across water obstacles. Introduced in 1960, it was followed by an improved version, the BMK-130M, in 1965. This had recesses in the hull for the wheels to fold into, reducing drag and the chance of wheel damage when in the water.

SPECIFICATIONS: BMK-130M

Crew: 2
Weight: 3,450kg
Length: 7.85m
Beam: 2.1m
Depth: 1.5m
Draught: 0.62m
Maximum speed: 21km/hour
Endurance: 12 hours
Towing power (forward): 1,450kg
Towing power (reverse): 800 tonnes

BMK-150

The BMK-150 was normally towed by a ZIL-131 6x6 3.5-tonne or ZIL-157 6x6 2.5-tonne lorry. The hull was made of aluminium, making it significantly lighter than the BMK-130. It had two screws, controlled by a pair of engines. A pair of integrated wheels meant that no trailer was required, simplifying launching. Once in the water, the wheels were folded back, and lay outside the hull. A petrol engine drove the boat at speeds of up to 22km/hour on the water. Unlike the BMK-130, it had a windscreen and a cover for protection against inclement weather. A seating area in the back allowed the boat to be used as a ferry for infantry.

The later BMK-150M had improved performance, and added wells in the hull to accommodate the wheels when they were folded back.

Specifications: BMK-150

Crew: 2
Weight: 2,500kg
Length: 8.2m
Beam: 2.55m
Depth: 2m
Draught: 0.66m
Maximum speed: 22km/hour
Endurance: 7 hours
Towing power (forward): 1,500kg

Specifications: BMK-150M

Crew: 2
Weight: 3,800kg
Length: 7.4m
Beam: 2.55m
Draught: 0.75m
Maximum speed: 22km/hour
Endurance: 6 hours

BMK-T

The BMK-T was introduced to replace the earlier BMK boats. Unlike earlier designs, it did not have integrated wheels. Instead, it was carried on the back of a KrAZ-214 6x6 7-tonne or KrAZ-255V 6x6 7.5-tonne lorry. It had a fully enclosed crew cabin and engine compartment, allowing it to operate in rough water. A large area at the back could be used to transport up to 25 fully equipped infantrymen.

Steering was done by turning the two propellers, rather than using rudders, making the boat very manoeuvrable. The propellers would automatically lift out of the water if an obstacle was encountered. The 180hp diesel engine powered the boat at speeds of up to 17km/hour. The boat could be remotely controlled at a distance of up to 30m. A powerful bilge pump was fitted, which could be used as a hose to extinguish fires or wash down pontoons, as well as evacuating water from the boat itself.

The boat was launched by gravity, often with the engine already running. Recovery was affected using a winch mounted on the lorry, pulling the boat over runners onto the rear bed. When travelling, the propellers were swung onto the top of the boat.

BMK-T on a KrAZ-260 lorry

SPECIFICATIONS: BMK-T

Crew: 2
Weight: 6 tonnes
Length: 8.6m
Beam: 2.7m
Depth: 2.2m
Draught: 0.75m
Maximum speed: 17km/hour
Endurance: 15-17 hours
Towing power (forward): 2,000kg
Towing power (reverse): 750 tonnes

BB-120 (DDR)

The BB-120 was essentially an East German copy of the Soviet BMK-90. The BB-120 differed in having no hand rails on the sides and a spray rail at the rear. It had a three-bladed propeller and a standard rudder. On land, it was carried on a four-wheel flatbed trailer.

Specifications: BB-120

Crew: 2
Weight: 3,500kg (without fuel)
Length: 7.85m
Beam: 2.1m
Depth: 1.5m
Draught: 0.55m
Maximum speed: 22km/hour
Towing power (forward): 1,200kg
Towing power (reverse): 700kg

KH-200 (Poland)

Development of the KH-200 started in the late 1960s, and it was approved for production in 1971. The hull was made of steel, with a cabin for the crew toward the front. Behind the cabin was a large open area, which could accommodate up to 15 troops, allowing the KH-200 to be used as a troop transport.

KH-200 being towed by a Ural-375 lorry

The engine drove a single propeller, with a top speed of 25km/hour. The KH-200 was used with the PP-64 pontoon bridge, and was transported on a two-axle trailer.

Specifications: KH-200

Crew: 2-3
Weight: 3,865kg
Length: 8.14m
Beam: 2.3m
Draught: 0.72m
Maximum speed: 25km/hour
Endurance: 12 hours
Towing power (forward): 2,500kg
Towing power (reverse): 1,200kg

Mo-108, Mo-111, Mo-930 (Czechoslovakia)

Czechoslovakia produced three bridging boats during the Cold War. The Mo-108 and Mo-111 were modifications of a German Second World War design, introduced in the 1950s. The only difference between the two was the engine. The Mo-111's engine was larger and more powerful, giving it a better performance. Both boats had three rudders and a single screw in a metal ring guard known as a Kort nozzle. They were transported on two-wheeled trailers, designated MP-4.

The later Mo-930 used the same engine as the Tatra 813 8x8 8-tonne lorry. Like the earlier boats, it had a single propeller and was transported on a two-wheel trailer. It was larger and heavier than the Mo-111, but had a more powerful engine, giving a similar performance.

SPECIFICATIONS: MO-111

Crew: 2
Weight: 3,200kg
Length: 7.5m
Beam: 2.2m
Depth: 1.2m
Draught: 0.85m
Maximum speed: 24km/hour

SPECIFICATIONS: MO-930

Crew: 2
Weight: 4 tonnes
Length: 7.68m
Beam: 2.2m
Draught: 0.85m
Maximum speed: 20km/hour
Endurance: 7 hours
Towing power (forward): 2,275kg
Towing power (reverse): 1,200kg

LINE OF COMMUNICATION BRIDGES

As well as bridging systems for use close to the front lines, considerable effort was put into the issue of bridges further behind the lines. During the Second World War, Soviet engineers built large bridges from scratch, using timber. After the war, pre-fabricated wooden bridges were developed. These required timber supports, but were still faster to construct. Supporting machinery, such as mobile cranes and specialised laying machines, were also developed.

The Warsaw Pact nations also used heavy barges to construct bridges. These would be lined up, either end to end or side to side, so that it was possible for a vehicle to drive over the barges from one bank to the other. The end-to-end arrangement was most common, though some barges were fitted with supports to allow a roadway to be fitted when lined up side to side. The barges could also be used to support tracks to create a railway bridge. These barge bridges were slow to construct, and blocked normal river traffic, so dedicated bridges and ferries were preferred where possible.

In the late 1980s, an underwater pontoon bridge set was introduced. The pontoons were similar to those used by the PMP bridge, and the bridge was constructed in a similar manner. When the bridge was complete, the pontoons were flooded, so that the bridge lay just under the water, making it difficult to spot.

PVM, LVM, TVM Suspension Bridges

These three bridges were developed primarily for use in mountainous areas. They were usually transported by pack animals, but could be carried on lorries if the terrain permitted.

The PVM was a foot bridge, and could be built as a single 120m bridge or two 60m bridges. In both cases, the bridge was 0.7m wide. An 18-man team took two hours to construct a single long bridge, or three hours to construct two shorter bridges. The set weighed a total of 4,360kg and could be carried by 46 pack animals.

The LVM set built 2m-wide bridges, one of 80m length or two of 40m length. They would take a team of 27 men two or four hours to build. The complete set weighed 13.5 tonnes and was transported on 160 pack animals. The completed bridge had a load capacity of 2 tonnes, but the axle load of any vehicle using it had to be no more than 635kg. The TVM was similar, but with a length of 60m and a load capacity of 10 tonnes.

MARM

The MARM light sectional bridge was used to cross dry gaps or rivers, and was often used as a road overpass to ease congestion at busy junctions. Each span was 6m long and included a set of adjustable-height folding trestles. The spans were put into place with a lorry-mounted crane, and the trestles braced. Spans were transported in pairs on semi-trailers towed by ZIL-130V tractor units. The MARM had a load capacity of 50 tonnes. A 118m bridge would take around eight hours to construct.

SARM

The SARM medium sectional deck truss bridge was made up of sections bolted together, with a roadway of steel deck panels. It could be built with a 4.2m-wide single roadway, having a capacity of 40 tonnes, or a 7.2m-wide dual roadway of 20 tonnes capacity. Each individual span could be 18.6m, 25.6m, or 32.6m long. Existing piers were used whenever possible.

Components were carried on single-axle semi-trailers towed by MAZ-504 or ZIL-130V tractor units. No individual pieces weighed more than 4.4 tonnes, so a 5-tonne crane was sufficient for construction. A 200m bridge would take 24 to 30 hours to construct.

BARM

This was a heavy pre-fabricated road bridge. It had a 60-tonne load, but could take special loads of up to 90 tonnes. Each span could be up to 52.5m long, and a set included two spans, an

8.84m-high pier, and installation and ancillary equipment. It took 24 hours to construct.

NZhM-56

The NZhM-56 was developed as a replacement for the wartime SP-19 bridge. The earlier bridge could carry road or rail traffic, but the NZhM-56 could carry both simultaneously.

A pontoon bridge, the NZhM-56 pontoons were in three sections: bow, centre, and stern. Each section was carried on a ZIL-131 6x6 3.5-tonne or ZIL-157 6x6 2.5-tonne lorry, with a trailer to accommodate the length of the pontoon section. Originally launched by crane, a later development allowed the pontoons to be launched by gravity. Once in the water, the sections were joined up, superstructure added, and the pontoons were pushed into position by boats.

NZhM-56 pontoon

The two-level superstructure included a roadway on the lower level and a railway on the upper level. The railway could be built to Soviet gauge (1.524m track) or European gauge (1.435m track). The roadway had a wooden deck on I-beam stringers with a capacity of 40 tonnes.

RMM-4

The RMM-4 portable fixed bridge was developed in the late 1940s. It could be used to repair destroyed bridges or, with the addition of supports, could be used to construct longer bridges. A complete set included 24 intermediate and eight end sections, carried on 12 GAZ-63 4x4 2-tonne lorries. The bridge had a wooden deck and two to four steel trusses, depending on the required length and capacity. Once assembled, the section would be pushed into place, and ramps would be added to complete the bridge. An RMM-4 set could create a 16-tonne bridge of 34m length, a 30-tonne bridge of 25m length, or a 60-tonne bridge of 16m length.

REM-500

The REM-500 was a sectional railway bridge, which could also function as a road bridge if a wooden floor was added. It consisted of 12.51m-long spans with integrated trestles. Each span weighed 10.7 tonnes, and the trestles could be adjusted from 3m to 12.7m. The railway track could be built to Soviet gauge (1.524m track) or European gauge (1.435m track). It was constructed a span at a time, using an overhead gantry (the SRK-2D) that travelled along the bridge as it was built. Trains had to slow to 30km/hour when crossing the bridge, with a maximum axle load of 20 tonnes.

SP-19 Self-Propelled Pontoon Bridge

A combination road and railway bridge introduced in 1939, the SP-19 saw use throughout the Second World War, and was replaced by the NZhM-56. Although it could be used to carry road or railway traffic, it could only carry one or the other, unlike the NZhM-56, which could carry both simultaneously.

An individual pontoon had a capacity of 22 tonnes. When formed into a ferry, the ferry had a capacity of 100 tonnes. A bridge could have a capacity of up to 180 tonnes, or sacrifice capacity for length, allowing a maximum length of 1,140m with a capacity of 30 tonnes.

TMS (Czechoslovakia)

The TMS was a heavy truss panel bridge. It was a double-truss, single-storey bridge, with a capacity of 100 tonnes and a span of 45m.

MS-1 (Czechoslovakia)

Sometimes referred to as the SM-60, the MS-1 was a single-storey heavy panel bridge with a 4m-wide roadway and a 60-tonne load capacity. Each span could be up to 21m long, and trestles could be used to make a multi-span bridge. The trestles had large baseplates to minimise ground pressure, and could be adjusted for heights of 1.5m to 7m. Cranes were required to construct the bridge, which was carried on TATRA 111 6x6 10-tonne lorries.

DMS-65 (POLAND)

The DMS-65 could be seen as an improved version of the venerable British Bailey bridge. It was usually built as a road bridge, but could also be built as a railway bridge. It had five basic elements, and could be constructed by manpower alone, or with the aid of cranes. Single or multi-span bridges could be built. The roadway consisted of metal sheets that could be optionally covered with crushed stone. The bridge was normally carried on Star 66 6x6 2.5-tonne lorries.

ESB-16 (DDR)

The ESB-16 railway-road bridge had both civilian and military variants, and could take European and Soviet-gauge railway track. Each span was 16m long, with a 4m-wide roadway, and made up of hollow box girders with cross-pieces. Nine trestles were provided, which could be adjusted to heights from 1.65m to 11.5m in 1cm intervals. The trestles had large, 7m2 rectangular bases. An SRK-50 crane was normally used to construct the bridge, though smaller cranes could be used if necessary.

SBG-66 (DDR)

Another bridge intended for both civilian and military use, the SBG-66 could be built on pontoons or fixed supports. It could be built as a road or railway bridge, and with fixed supports could be built as a jetty or overpass. It had a load capacity of 80 tonnes, and could have a single 4m-wide roadway or a 7m-wide, two-lane roadway. The pontoons were 32.5m long, 8.2m wide, and positioned by boats.

SB-30 AND SB-45 (DDR)

The SB-30 road bridge was designed to be compatible with existing bridging, but faster to construct and easier to maintain. SB-30 spans were 30m long with a load capacity of 60 tonnes, a single roadway width of 4.2m or double roadway width of 7.75m. Individual elements were made of corrosion-resistant steel, 7.5m long and 10 tonnes in weight.

Tests revealed that for wheeled vehicles, including tank transporters, the spans could be lengthened to 45m. The use of longer spans resulted in significantly reduced construction times, since fewer supports were needed. This resulted in a new version, the SB-45, which could have spans 30m, 37.5m, or 45m long. Load capacities were 80 tonnes, 60 tonnes, and 40 tonnes respectively. With a double-lane bridge used as a single lane, loads of up to 86 tonnes could cross 45m spans. If the spans were reduced to 22.5m it could carry railway traffic.

Mine Warfare

The Soviet army considered mines to be an important part of both offensive and defensive warfare. There are no precise figures for the number of mines deployed in Afghanistan, but it is estimated to be in the millions. It is known that when the Soviets withdrew, they handed over records of 613 minefields to the Afghan army.

Minelaying

The traditional method of laying mines by hand was time-consuming, labour-intensive, and vulnerable. The Soviet army therefore developed equipment that allowed vehicles to lay mines quickly. Initially, these were simple chutes that could be attached to the side of a lorry or APC. Mines would drop down the chute by gravity, to lay on the surface, possibly to be buried by a follow-on team. These evolved into the more advanced PMR-2 and PMR-3 remotely-delivered mines (also known as scatterable mines). These could be deployed by helicopter, aircraft, artillery (tube or rocket), or missile.

Remotely-delivered mines were used in large quantities in Afghanistan. They were used to interdict mujahideen lines of communication and supply, and to block escape routes during attacks. Multiple-launch rocket systems were generally favoured for delivering mines, since they could cover a large area in a short time.

Helicopter Minelaying Equipment

Warsaw Pact armies deployed minelaying chutes on Mi-4 and Mi-8 helicopters. The Mi-4 could carry 200 mines, while the Mi-8 could carry 400. Both could lay mines on the surface at a rate of four per minute. The introduction of the very small PFM-1 "butterfly" mine allowed over 7,000 mines to be carried by a single helicopter. Very many of these mines were dispensed by helicopter in Afghanistan.

GMZ and GMZ-2

The GMZ tracked minelayer entered service in the mid-late 1960s. It is based on the SU-100P chassis, a prototype tank destroyer that never entered full production. It was fitted with infra-red driving lights, an NBC protection system, and could generate smoke by injecting diesel fuel into the exhaust. It had a 14.5mm KPVT heavy machine gun for self-defence.

Preparing the mines would take 15 to 40 minutes. Once this was done, the vehicle would be driven at a speed of up to 16km/hour if the mines were to be laid on top of the ground. If the mines were to be buried, it would drive at about 3km/hour. Mines would be fed onto trays on top of the vehicle. If the mines were to be buried, a plough would lift the ground. The mines would be automatically placed on the ground or inside the ploughed trough.

The GMZ-2 was an improved model. It had a more powerful engine, and allowed for different fuse types to be fitted to the mines.

GMZ-2

Specifications: GMZ

Crew: 4
Weight: 25 tonnes
Length: 9.1m (travelling)
Length: 10.3m (operating)
Width: 3.1m
Height: 2.5m
Maximum road speed: 50km/hour
Gradient: 60%
Vertical obstacle: 10.3m
Operating speed: 4-10km/hour (surface mines)
Operating speed: 2-3km/hour (buried mines)
Minelaying rate: 8 mines/minute (surface mines)
Minelaying rate: 4 mines/minute (buried mines)
Mine spacing: 4-5.5m
Reload time: 12-15 minutes

GMZ-3

Unlike the earlier vehicles in the series, the GMZ-3 was based on the SA-4 chassis. The driver and vehicle commander were seated at the front, with the engine to their right. A land-navigation system was fitted, and the driver had infra-red night vision, allowing minelaying operations to be conducted at night. The commander also had infra-red night vision equipment, and operated the PKT machine gun. Smoke dischargers were fitted on the side of the superstructure, at the rear. Unlike the earlier models, it could not generate smoke by injecting diesel into the exhaust.

GMZ-3, showing the mine-laying mechanism

The mine stowage and laying equipment was at the rear of the vehicle. 208 mines were carried, loaded into the vehicle through a pair of large roof hatches. When laying mines, they were fed into two chutes, one on each side. The laying system could bury mines up to 12cm deep in soil or 50cm deep in snow. When laying mines on the surface, they were laid at a rate of up to eight per minute at a speed of 6 to 16km/hour. When laying buried mines, the rate was halved, and the maximum speed reduced to 6km/hour.

Specifications: GMZ-3

Crew: 3
Weight: 28.5 tonnes
Length: 8.62m (travelling)
Width: 3.25m
Height: 2.7m (travelling)
Ground clearance: 0.45m
Maximum road speed: 60km/hour
Maximum road range: 500km
Gradient: 58%
Vertical obstacle: 0.7m
Operating speed: 6-16km/hour (surface mines)
Operating speed: 6km/hour (buried mines)
Minelaying rate: 8 mines/minute (surface mines)
Minelaying rate: 4 mines/minute (buried mines)
Mine spacing: 5-10m
Reload time: 15-20 minutes
Armament: 7.62mm PKT MG

PMR-2, PMR-3, and PMZ-4

The PMR-2 was a two-wheel trailer with a pair of chutes. The chutes were wide at the top, where mines were loaded. Mines rolled down a conveyor to the laying mechanism. In the PMR-2, mines were laid on the surface, and could be buried by a follow-on team if required.

The PMR-3 had a single chute, but added a plough which allowed mines to be laid on the surface or buried up to 30 to

PMR-3

40cm deep in soft soil. The PMZ-4 was identical, but the capacity was increased from 120 to 200 mines.

All three were usually towed behind a BTR-152, but could also be towed behind an unarmoured lorry or a BTR-60 armoured personnel carrier. Capacity was increased when towed behind a lorry, up to 350 mines when towed by a Ural-375 6x6 4.5-tonne lorry.

SPECIFICATIONS: PMR-3

Crew: 4 or 5
Length: 3.25m
Width: 2m
Height: 2.5m
Operating speed: 4-10km/hour (surface mines)
Operating speed: 2-3km/hour (buried mines)
Minelaying rate: 10-12 mines/minute

Mine spacing: 4-5.5m
Reload time: 10-12 minutes

UMZ

Adopted in the late 1970s, the UMZ scatterable minelayer consisted of six rotating launcher units mounted on the back of a ZIL-131 6x6 3.5-tonne lorry. Each launcher unit had 30 firing tubes. Mines were fitted into cylindrical cassettes, which were then loaded into the firing tubes. Depending on the type of mine, up to 64 mines could be fitted into each cassette, giving a total of up to 11,520 mines.

Mines were fired to a distance of 30 to 60m from the UMZ, with the vehicle driving at up to 40 km/hour. Minefields of varying widths and depths could be laid, depending on the elevation of the launcher units and speed of the vehicle. The UMZ had a crew of two, and reloading would take 1.5 to 2.5 hours, depending on the type of mines being loaded. With six men, reloading time was reduced to 40 to 60 minutes.

MLG-60 (DDR)

The East German MLG-60 was similar to the Soviet PMR-3. However, where the PMR-3 included a seat for the operator, with the MLG-60 the operator was seated inside the towing vehicle. The MLG-60 also added a large twin follow-up scraper on the rear of the trailer. Mines could be laid on the surface or buried, with spacing between 4m and 6m. It was normally towed by a 6x6 lorry or BTR-152 APC. A slightly improved model, the MLG-60M, was introduced later.

Specifications: MLG-60

Crew: 2
Weight: 800kg
Length: 4.9m (travelling)
Length: 5.9m (operating)
Width: 1.87m
Height: 1.95m (travelling)
Height: 2.1m (operating)
Operating speed: 3-5km/hour

Mine Detection

Various Warsaw Pact armies experimented with the use of helicopter-mounted mine detectors. The detection assembly would be slung under a helicopter, which would fly over a suspected minefield. Once the presence of a minefield, and its extent, had been determined, breaching operations could be carried out.

In addition to mine detectors, the Soviet army made extensive use of mine-sniffer dogs in Afghanistan. They were particularly useful for detecting non-metallic mines. Although they gave good service, they would have been of less use in a highly mobile campaign such as was expected in Western Europe.

VIM-625 and VIM-695 Portable Mine Detectors

Developed during the Second World War, these had a rubber-insulated search head, a search handle, a tuning box, a battery box, and headphones. The battery box, carried in a backpack, contained a 2.8V and a 60V battery. The complete equipment weighed 13kg and could be operated for 10 hours.

VIM-203M Metallic Mine Detector

Developed during the Second World War, the VIM-203M worked on the beat frequency oscillation principle. Two models were used, one with a circular search coil and separate tuning box, the other with a square search coil and a tuning box mounted on the rear of the coil. The former model was heavier (13.5kg), with a higher battery voltage and operating time of 30 hours.

UMIV-1 Portable Mine Detector

Introduced after the Second World War, the UMIV-1 had a rectangular detector at the end of a cylindrical metal handle. A backpack contained the control box and headset. The handle was made up of four pieces, two of which were detachable. It could detect metallic objects at depths of up to 450mm.

Specifications: UMIV-1

Weight: 6.6kg
Detector head size: 220x146mm
Detection range: 450mm
Handle length: 660-1300mm

IMP Portable Mine Detector

The IMP had a cylindrical detector at the end of a four-piece aluminium handle, headphones, and a tuning box combined with battery pack. For working in confined spaces, some pieces of the handle could be removed. With all four handles fitted, the handle was 1.58m long. The detector had two transmitting antennae and one receiving antenna in a Bakelite case. Detection range was up to 460mm.

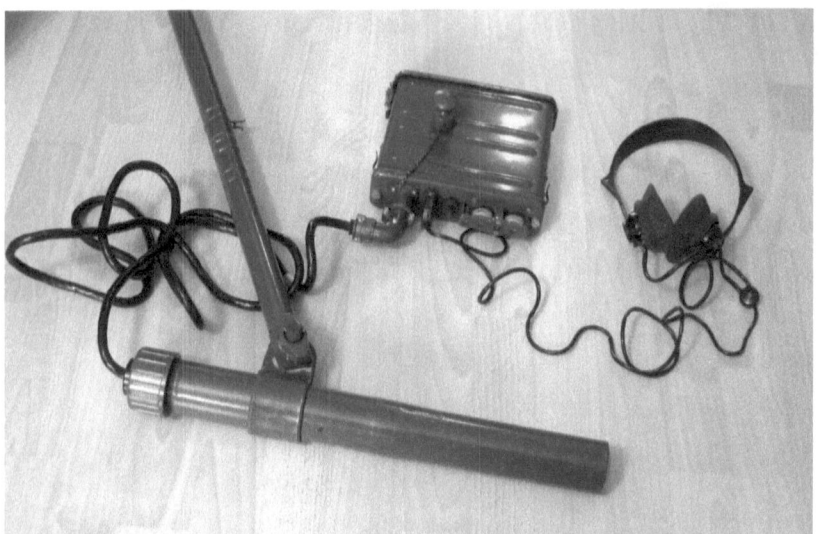

IMP mine detector

The IMP could detect metal mines and plastic mines with some metal components. When disassembled, the IMP was carried in a lightweight, rectangular metal box. It could be used underwater up to a depth of 1m.

SPECIFICATIONS: IMP

Weight: 9.7kg
Detection range: 460mm
Detector head diameter: 38mm
Detector head length: 417mm

DIM VEHICLE-MOUNTED MINE DETECTOR

This mine detector was normally fitted to a GAZ-69 or UAZ-469 4x4 light vehicle. In Afghanistan, the unarmoured vehicles were found to be vulnerable to sniper fire, so they were fitted to T-62 tanks instead. The DIM consisted of a non-magnetic sensing head mounted on a frame. The frame had a pair of rubber-tyred wheels behind the sensing head, which ran along the road surface when in use. When in transit, the assembly was rotated back to rest on top of the vehicle.

When in use, the vehicle was driven at up to 10km/hour, and would detect mines at a depth of up to 250mm. When a mine was detected, an alarm sounded and the vehicle's brakes were automatically applied. The operator could then adjust the search coils to determine the exact location of the mine.

VISF Model 1946 Portable Mine Detector (Bulgaria)

An improved version of the Soviet VIM-203M. It had a rectangular search head assembly with the amplifier box mounted on it. The search handle was made up of four wooden pieces, and could be adjusted with extension pieces. The tone regulator was mounted on the top section of the search handle, and a cast iron battery box was attached at the end of the same section. It was a good deal lighter than the Soviet model (6.2kg), doubled the detection range.

M62 Portable Mine Detector (Bulgaria)

This handheld mine detector could detect metallic mines or plastic mines with metal components. The rectangular detector head was mounted on a search handle, which contained the power source and operating controls. It could detect a 300mm-diameter metallic object at a 500mm distance. It weighed 2.5kg.

M-10 and M-11 Portable Mine Detectors (Czechoslovakia)

These two handheld mine detectors were very similar, but with different search head designs. Both operated on the beat frequency oscillation principle. The M-10 had two detachable, 300mm-diameter plates, while the M-11 had a single plate, with the same effective area. The handle was made up of four jointed sections, each 500mm long. A canvas pack contained the tuning box and batteries. Both weighed 12kg, and were carried in a canvas backpack.

MSG 64 Portable Mine Detector (DDR)

This handheld mine detector had an oval detector assembly and three-piece search handle. The handle contained the tuning box, tone regulator, and batteries. It could detect a 50mm-diameter metallic object at a 180mm distance. It could be disassembled for carrying in a camouflaged waterproof canvas case. The angle of the waterproof detector head was adjustable. It weighed 4.4kg.

Specifications: MSG 64

Weight: 4.4kg
Detection range: 180mm
Handle length: 2.4mm
Detector head weight: 2.35kg

Mine Clearance

The Warsaw Pact armies made extensive use of mine rollers and ploughs in the early part of the Cold War. These were very heavy, requiring cranes for fitting and removal. The KM-61 crane, fitted on a KrAZ-214 6x6 7-tonne lorry, was developed for this task. It had a maximum capacity of 3.2 tonnes and a reach of 2m.

Although vehicles with mine rollers and mine ploughs were a huge improvement over foot troops with mine detectors, they presented a tempting target. Minefields would normally be covered by anti-tank weapons, which would focus on mine-clearing vehicles. In the 1970s, NATO introduced new mine systems such as the US FASCAM system. This enabled NATO commanders to lay remote minefields rapidly, markedly increasing the mine threat. Experiments with explosive-breaching systems, which would allow minefields to be cleared much more quickly, had already begun in the 1960s. The MTK was the first operational system to result from these experiments.

PT-54, PT-54M, AND PT-55 MINE ROLLERS

Introduced during the 1950s, the PT-54 replaced the Second World War-era PT-3 mine rollers. The PT-54 used smaller rollers than the PT-3, in an improved mounting. The PT-54, PT-54M, and PT-55 all worked in the same way. All three consisted of sets of rollers with serrated edges, positioned in front of the host tank's tracks. These rollers would detonate any mines, and also cut a 100mm-wide furrow, marking the safe track for other tanks to follow. A weighted chain between the rollers detonated tilt-rod fused mines before the hull of the tank passed over them.

The PT-54 had six rollers in each set. This was reduced to five per set in the PT-54M, and four per set in the PT-55. Reducing the number of rollers meant that the cleared lane was narrower, but the tank could move faster whilst clearing. All three required a crane to fit, which took around 10 to 15 minutes. Removal time was three to five minutes. A set of rollers had to be replaced after 10 anti-tank mines had been swept. Since the area between the tracks was not swept, three tanks would usually operate in a wedge pattern.

Czechoslovakia used their own version of the Soviet mine rollers. The Czech designs were similar, but with larger rollers, a different design of serrated edge, and a frame instead of a chain to detonate tilt-rod fused mines.

SPECIFICATIONS: PT-54

Weight: 8.8 tonnes
Lane width: 1.3m
Operating speed: 6-10km/hour
Attachment time: 10-15 minutes

SPECIFICATIONS: PT-54M

Weight: 7 tonnes
Lane width: 0.89m
Attachment time: 10-25 minutes

SPECIFICATIONS: PT-55

Weight: 6.7 tonnes
Lane width: 1.7m
Operating speed: 8-12km/hour
Attachment time: 10-15 minutes

KMT-4 MINE PLOUGH

The Warsaw Pact armies found that mine rollers had some significant disadvantages. They were heavy, and significantly reduced the host tank's mobility, especially over rough ground.

The extra weight reduced the life of the tank's transmission and power plant. In addition, advances in fuse design meant that mines would not always be detonated by rollers. The KMT-4 mine plough was introduced in the 1960s to address these issues.

The KMT-4 was the first plough design used by the Warsaw Pact armies. It had a 600mm-wide cutting device in front of each track, with five teeth mounted at an angle. In transit, the blades were kept above ground, allowing the tank to travel at full speed. When in use, the blades were lowered to the ground by a hydraulic ram, and the tank would move at a maximum speed of 12km/hour. As the tank moved forward, the plough would dig up any buried mines and deposit them to the side of the tank's path.

The KMT-4M, which had improvements to the blade attachment system, was introduced in the late 1960s.

KMT-5 Mine Plough and Rollers

The KMT-5 was introduced in the mid-1960s. It combined a KMT-4 mine plough with two sets of three rollers. The individual rollers were thicker than those on the PT-55, and cleared roughly the same width. It was only possible to use both plough and rollers on good, flat ground. Usually one or the other would be used, depending on ground conditions. When used together, the plough was fitted behind the rollers, so that it would clear mines that were not detonated by the rollers. Despite having both rollers and ploughs, the weight was not a great deal more than that of the PT-55, and less than that of the earlier PT-54. The device took 30 to 45 minutes to attach, and could be operated at a speed of 12 to 18km/hour, depending on ground conditions.

An improved version, the KMT-5M, was introduced in the late 1960s. This added a lane-marking plough and the PSK marking system, which used a luminescent substance and flares to mark the cleared lane. Romania made their own copy of the KMT-5M, designated the D-5M.

SPECIFICATIONS: KMT-5

Weight: 7.5 tonnes
Lane width: 0.81m

KMT-6 Mine Plough

Introduced in the late 1960s, the KMT-6 was an improved version of the KMT-4M. Originally developed for use with the T-64 tank, it was also used with the T-72 and T-80. Each plough cleared a path 750mm wide, with a gap of 1.9m.

KMT-7 Mine Plough and Rollers

The KMT-7 was similar to the earlier KMT-5, but with some improvements, and mountings suitable for use with the T-64, T-72, and T-80 tanks. The frames for the rollers allowed more vertical movement, reducing the effect of a blast on the rollers. The KMT-7 could clear two tracks of 1.65m width at a speed of 6-12km/hour. As with earlier systems, fitting required a crane, but the tank driver could disconnect the system using explosive squibs. This allowed the tank to drive away and continue as a combat vehicle.

KMT-8 Mine Plough

Similar to the KMT-7, this was intended for use with all Soviet main battle tanks, and the IMR-2 combat engineer vehicle.

Pneumatic cylinders raised and lowered the ploughs. Once lowered, sensors kept the ploughs at the optimum depth, and each plough could clear a path 600mm wide. The plough units were connected by a metal rod to detonate tilt-rod fused mines.

Installation took around 90 minutes, and once fitted, the tank's performance was not affected. A single set could plough for up to 30km, at speeds of up to 15km/hour, before requiring repair.

SPECIFICATIONS: KMT-8

Weight: 1.2 tonnes
Lane width: 0.6m
Operating speed: 15km/hour
Attachment time: 90 minutes

KMT-10 MINE PLOUGH

Unlike the other mine ploughs described in this section, the KMT-10 was not used with tanks. Rather, it was developed for use with the BMP-1 and BMP-2 infantry fighting vehicles. This necessitated it being much smaller and lighter than the other ploughs.

As with the tank ploughs, rods were fitted between the ploughs to detonate tilt-rod fused mines. Since the BMP's armour was thin, an extra plate of armour was provided to be fitted to the lower front, to provide protection from detonating mines. The BMP could travel at a speed of 6 to 15km/hour while clearing mines. Each cleared lane was 300mm wide, with a gap of 2.4m between lanes.

MTK Armoured Mine-Clearing Vehicle

The MTK was the first result of the experiments with rocket-breaching mine systems, begun in the 1960s. Based on the BTR-50PK armoured personnel carrier, it carried a UR-67 rocket launcher system. The rocket was attached to a 170m length of UZR-3 high-explosive triple line charge. The vehicle was driven to the edge of a minefield, the rocket's launcher at the rear of the hull was elevated, and the rocket fired. The rocket pulled the line charge across the minefield. The crew then used a line towed behind the line charge to position the charges for maximum effect. Once it was in place, the charge was detonated, clearing any mines in the vicinity.

MTK-2 Armoured Mine-Clearing Vehicle

The MTK-2 entered service in the early 1980s, based on the 2S1 self-propelled howitzer chassis. A low superstructure housed three UR-77 rockets and their launch ramps. Before firing, the launch ramps and the upper part of the superstructure were raised hydraulically. Each rocket towed a pair of 93m-long UZ-67 or UZP-77 high-explosive line charge. The UZ-67 could be used over ranges of 200 to 350m, while the UZP-77 could be used over ranges of 200 to 500m.

A cable connected the line charges to the vehicle. After firing, the vehicle would manoeuvre to position the line charges for greatest effect before detonating the charges. The charges would clear a path 6 to 8m wide and 75 to 80m (UZ-67) or 80 to 90m (UZP-77) long. The whole operation would take three to five minutes, without any need for the crew to exit the vehicle. The MTK-2 had NBC protection for the crew of two, and was amphibious.

Specifications: MTK-2

Crew: 2
Weight: 15.5 tonnes
Length: 7.26m
Width: 2.85m
Height: 3.91m
Maximum road speed: 61.5km/hour

ITB-2, SPZ-2, and SPZ-4

The ITB-2 was a rocket-launched anchor and cable, launched across a minefield. The cable was then used to draw a linear explosive charge across the minefield, usually using a winch. Once the charge was in position, it was detonated to clear a path.

The SPZ-2 used a metal-framed anchor to winch a cable with explosive charge across the area to be cleared, at a speed of up to 200m/hour. Single, double, and triple charges were available, and would clear a path up to 500m long and 6m wide.

The SPZ-4 was a double or triple charge, used with tanks. It could be pushed onto the minefield at a rate of up to 100m/hour. If the tank had a mine-clearing plough or roller, it could be towed behind the tank, to clear the gap between the paths cleared by the plough or roller.

BDT

The BDT was a mine-clearing charge in a 305mm-long, 50mm-diameter light metal tube. It contained three linear charges connected in parallel to form a triple charge, but could be disassembled to form single or double charges. Charges were connected end to end, to create a charge of the desired length, up to about 500m. A squad of men would take 60 to 90 minutes to create a 500m-long charge.

Once the charge had been made up to the required length, the detonator was added. A roller was then fitted to the front, to allow the charge to be pushed into place. A shield was also added, to prevent enemy fire causing a premature detonation. The charge would be assembled to the rear, then towed to the minefield and pushed into place by an armoured vehicle, at a speed of up to 10km/hour. Once in place, the charge was detonated, to clear a 6m-wide path.

UZ-1 and UZ-2 Bangalore Torpedoes

Bangalore torpedoes were used to clear paths through minefields and barbed wire. The UZ-1 was a metal tube, 1m long and 53mm in diameter, with 5.3kg of explosive. The UZ-2 was 2m long, 52mm in diameter, with 3.3kg of explosive. Both types were intended to be connected in series to the required length.

Once assembled, the torpedo would be pushed onto the minefield or into the barbed wire, then detonated to clear a path around 3m wide. Special collars were provided which would allow the torpedoes to be connected as double or triple charges, to clear a wider path. A metal shield was sometimes fitted to the front of the complete charge to prevent enemy small-arms fire causing a premature explosion.

PW-LWD (Poland)

Like the MTK, this was a system based around the UR-67 rocket launcher and UZR-3 line charge. It consisted of two bathtub-shaped containers, each containing a rocket and 110m of line charge. The container roofs were raised to allow the rockets to be fired. Once the rocket had towed the line charge over the minefield, the charge was detonated. The charge would clear a path 4m wide and up to 110m long.

The equipment was carried on a T-55A or T-72 tank, or an IWT combat engineer vehicle. When fitted to a tank, a standard mine plough and lane-marking equipment were also fitted.

SPECIFICATIONS: PW-LWD

Weight: 920kg (line charge)
Weight: 230kg (launcher)
Length: 110m (line charge)
Length: 2.82m (launcher)
Width: 15.5m (launcher)
Height: 0.68m (launcher)

TANK-MOUNTED ROLLERS AND PLOUGHS (CZECHOSLOVAKIA)

The Czech army used tank-mounted mine-clearing rollers and ploughs rather than Soviet designs. The roller system had three to five rollers of varying thicknesses mounted on an arm in front of each track, in a similar way to the Soviet systems. The Czech designs were larger, with a different type of serrated edge. A frame was mounted between and in front of the rollers to detonate tilt-rod fused mines.

The plough equipment was similar to the Soviet equivalents, though larger. Like the rollers, it had a frame for detonating tilt-rod fused mines.

Trailer-based system (Czechoslovakia)

The Czech army developed a system very similar to the Polish PW-LWD, but mounted the containers on an armoured, four-wheel trailer. This was usually towed behind an OT-64 8x8 APC, and was used in the same way as the Polish system.

Armoured Engineer Vehicles

IMR Combat Engineer Vehicle

Developed from a prototype built in 1969, the IMR was based on the T-55 chassis. The turret was replaced by a hydraulic crane with full 360° traverse. The crane jib was telescopic, and when in transit, was turned to the rear and seated on a cradle. The cradle folded down against the hull when the crane was in use.

The crane was normally fitted with a pair of pincer grabs, but a small bucket was also provided, stowed above the left rear track when not in use. The operator was seated in an armoured cupola, and a searchlight on the crane allowed for use at night.

A hydraulic bulldozer blade was fitted to the front hull. This blade could be used in the straight or V configuration, but could not be used in the angle configuration. An unditching beam was fitted at the rear of the hull.

The Polish army used a variant, designated IWT. It was basically the same vehicle, but could be fitted with a PW-LWD mine-clearing line charge system.

Specifications: IMR

Crew: 2
Weight: 37.5 tonnes
Length: 10.6m
Width: 3.27m
Height: 3.37m
Ground clearance: 0.43m
Maximum road speed: 48km/hour
Maximum road range: 400km
Gradient: 60%
Vertical obstacle: 0.8m

Armour:
Hull front: 100mm @ 60° [Effective: 200mm]
Hull sides: 70mm
Hull top: 30mm
Hull rear: 60mm
Belly: 20mm

IMR-2 Combat Engineer Vehicle

The IMR-2 replaced the IMR, and was based on a T-72 chassis. The turret was replaced by an armoured superstructure with armoured windows. A telescopic arm was fitted to the superstructure, with 360° traverse, 8.15m reach, and a lift capacity of 2 tonnes. This was normally fitted with a gripper-type manipulator, but could also be fitted with a bucket or shovel.

A set of KMT-8 mine ploughs were carried, and later models had a mine-clearing line charge system. A hydraulically operated bulldozer blade was fitted at the front, and folded upwards when not in use.

In 1982, the IMR-2M1 was introduced, which sacrificed the mine-clearing line charge in favour of greater protection for the hydraulic system. A new version, the IMR-2M2, was introduced in 1990. This had an improved manipulator for the telescopic arm.

All models had night-vision equipment for the driver and commander, NBC protection, and fire detection/suppression systems. They could all create smoke by injecting diesel fuel into the exhaust manifold.

Specifications: IMR-2

Crew: 2
Weight: 44.3 tonnes
Length: 9.55m
Width: 4.35m
Height: 3.68m
Ground clearance: 0.46m
Maximum road speed: 59km/hour
Maximum road range: 500km

IRM Engineer Reconnaissance Vehicle

Originally identified in the West as the IPR amphibious engineer vehicle, the IRM was based on the BMP-2's automotive components. It was intended to facilitate specialised engineering reconnaissance over a wide variety of terrain and climate conditions. It could be carried by cargo aircraft, assault ship, or hovercraft.

Although it used BMP-2 automotive components, the IRM had seven road wheels on each side, rather than the BMP-2's six, and five return rollers. It was fully amphibious, with a trim vane for use in the water, and was propelled in the water by a pair of propellers. It could also carry a 10m snorkel, to allow it to operate fully submerged.

The vehicle was divided into three internal compartments: the driver's compartment at the front, a fighting compartment in the centre, and the engine compartment at the rear. The crew compartments had NBC protection. The vehicle also had a bilge pump, a fire-extinguishing system, and could generate smoke by injecting diesel into the exhaust.

The basic crew consisted of driver and commander, both seated near the front, and each had a hatch in the roof. The commander also had a small turret, mounting a 7.62mm PKT machine gun and an infra-red searchlight. The vehicle normally carried one or two engineers, or up to four if required, for dismounted operations. The engineers also had roof hatches, and there was an emergency escape hatch at the bottom of the hull.

A variety of specialised engineering reconnaissance equipment was carried. This included a TNA-3 inertial navigation system, a mine detection system, and a sensor for determining the load-bearing capability of terrain. Equipment for reconnaissance of river crossing sites and beaches was fitted, including an artificial horizon and an inclinometer. An echo sounder and hydro-acoustic transducers were used to determine water depth and firmness of river beds. Day and night-vision devices were carried, along with an engineer reconnaissance periscope and a range finder. Portable equipment was carried for use by dismounted engineers. This included mine detectors, devices to measure the thickness of ice, and load-bearing measuring instruments.

For mine detection, a pair of arms were fitted which could be extended in front of the tracks. These had mine detectors, which

IRM

used a hydraulic terrain-following mechanism to keep a fixed distance above the ground. The vehicle stopped automatically if a mine was detected or if a detector struck an obstacle. The mine would then have to be removed manually.

The IRM was fitted with an innovative system to allow it to recover itself from difficult terrain. Two banks of rockets were fitted on the rear roof, which could be activated with the crew remaining inside the vehicle. These rockets would provide tractive force of 312kg each, to help the vehicle extract itself.

SPECIFICATIONS: IRM

Crew: up to 6
Weight: 17.2 tonnes
Length: 8.22m
Width: 3.15m
Height: 2.4m

Maximum road speed: 52km/hour

Maximum road range: 500km

Gradient: 36%

Vertical obstacle: 0.65m

Armament: 1x 7.62mm PKT MG

ADZM Engineer Vehicle

The ADZM was a combat engineer variant of the MT-LB. Only slightly modified from the standard vehicle, it was used by airborne brigades. It carried a plough blade, which was fitted on the hull side or roof for transit. Two hydraulic arm assemblies were added to the rear, to which the plough could be manually attached. There were no attachments to the front, so the blade could only be used to the rear. An arm with a bucket was mounted on the roof. Combat engineer equipment was carried inside the vehicle.

MT-LB Engineer Vehicles

The East German army used MT-LBs for combat engineering, but this version did not have a plough blade. It did have a rectangular box on the hull roof for engineering equipment. A Czech design named Zabot mounted a large bulldozer blade at the rear. This design never got past the prototype stage.

The Polish army used an engineer variant of the MT-LB which had been designed and produced in Poland. Intended primarily for engineering reconnaissance, it was fitted with a WAT turret (as fitted on the OT-64 and some OT-62 variants). This turret had a 14.5mm KPVT and a 7.62mm PKT machine gun. Eight smoke grenade dischargers were mounted on the hull sides, near the rear, four per side. These were mounted such that four fired forward, and four to the rear. The vehicle had a crew of two, and could carry up to six additional engineers. It was amphibious and had NBC protection.

Recovery and Repair Vehicles

The Soviet army had no armoured recovery vehicles during the Second World War. This was in marked contrast to the German army, which had developed specialised recovery vehicles and tactics for their use. Toward the end of the war, the Soviet army started to experiment with armoured recovery vehicles.

Some Western sources have identified an armoured recovery vehicle based on the "IT-130" tank destroyer. The IT-130 was said to mount a 130mm gun on a vehicle based on the T-62 tank. Little was known about this vehicle, although photographs were occasionally published. Since the IT-130 was later proved to be fictitious, it seems that the ARV variant did not actually exist.

T-34 ARVs

The Soviet army's initial experiments with ARVs were conversions of existing armoured vehicles with little or no specialised equipment. There was no standard design, but they were usually a T-34 with the turret removed. Shortly after the war, a standardised vehicle, the T-34-T, was produced. Like the wartime vehicles, this had no specialised equipment, being a T-34 with the turret opening plated over and a commander's cupola added. Units often added civilian winches and cranes to improve the vehicle's usefulness.

IS-T

As ISU assault guns started to be withdrawn from Soviet service in the late 1950s, some were used as the basis for heavy recovery vehicles. The initial examples simply had their guns removed, but most were rebuilt in one of two versions. One version had winches, a rear entrenching spade, and a stowage box over the rear hull. The other version had a simple, large A-frame crane fitted to the front, which was swung back to lay along the hull roof when not in use.

BTS-1

A number of armoured recovery vehicles were built based on the T-54 and T-55 chassis, and designated BTS (medium armoured tower) in the Soviet Union. The first, the BTS-1, was basically a turretless T-54, much like the earlier T-34-T. The driver sat at the front on the left, with the commander to his right. Other crew members sat in the rear cargo area, which also held a snorkel for deep wading. Tow bars of various lengths were carried, as was an unditching beam, carried on the right of the hull.

BTS-2

The BTS-2 was based on the BTS-1, but added a winch in the hull, and a container for tools and equipment. A 2-tonne capacity tripod jib crane was fitted, and a large entrenching spade was added to the rear. This spade could be used to anchor the vehicle when the winch was in use.

BTS-3

Introduced in the 1960s, the BTS-3 was based on a T-55 hull. It had a bulldozer blade at the front and a 20-tonne capacity crane on the right side of the hull. This crane had a telescopic jib, and was traversed to the rear, resting along the hull, when not in use.

T-54 (A) AND T-54 (B) (DDR)

Developed by the East German army, these differed from the T-54-T by not having a spade at the rear. They did have push-pull bars, welding and cutting equipment, and a dismountable 1-tonne crane. They were fitted with detectors to warn of radiation or chemical contamination, and had fittings for PT-54 or PT-55 mine rollers.

The T-54 (B) added brackets at the rear for securing tow ropes, and a protective plate on the front hull glacis.

BREM-64

Shortly after the introduction of the T-64 MBT, a new ARV was introduced, based on the new chassis. The turret was replaced by an armoured superstructure, which included a raised cupola for the commander. A 2.5-tonne capacity folding-jib crane was fitted on the superstructure, toward the left. Unlike the earlier T-54/55-based ARVs, the BREM-64 had two winches. The primary winch had a capacity of 25 tonnes, and a front-mounted bulldozer blade was used to anchor the vehicle when it was in use. The secondary winch had a capacity of 2.5 tonnes. As well as anchoring the vehicle, the bulldozer blade could be used to clear obstacles and prepare sites.

An auxiliary power unit was carried, which could be used to power dismounted power tools and welding equipment. The BREM-64 carried a 12.7mm NSVT machine gun, primarily for air defence, and had a crew of three: driver, gunner, and fitter.

BREM-1

Introduced in 1984, the BREM-1 was an ARV based on the T-72 MBT chassis. It had a crew of three (driver, commander, and mechanic), all of whom were provided with day and night-vision equipment. It had a top road speed of 60km/hour, a road range of 700km, and an off-road range of 500km. Towing another tank significantly reduced the range, to just 220km on roads. Like the main battle tank, it had long-range fuel drums at the rear of the vehicle, which could be jettisoned if needed. An unditching beam was mounted underneath the external fuel drums. A large-diameter snorkel was carried on the rear right of the vehicle, which could be used for deep wading at depths of up to 5m.

A crane was fitted on the left side of the vehicle. This had a lift capacity of 19 tonnes when extended up to 2m, or 3 tonnes at the maximum extension of 4.4m. The crane was powered hydraulically, normally using power from the vehicle's main engine to run the pump. If the main engine was not running, the vehicle batteries could power the crane via an electrical pump. The crane was controlled from an elevated position, with a full set of controls. The crane turntable could be locked, and the vehicle could travel over level ground with a load suspended from the crane. When in transit, the crane was folded down along the side of the vehicle and secured in place with a clamp.

A full set of electric welding equipment, including a working position, was carried in a hermetically-sealed panel over the left

BREM-1

track. Special tools were carried in portable containers on a load platform. This load platform was located at the centre of the roof, and was 1.7m long and 1.4m wide. It had removable side panels, and could carry a load of up to 1.5 tonnes.

The BREM-1 had two winches, a plough, a bulldozer blade, and towing equipment. The mechanical main winch had a 200m cable and a basic capacity of 25 tonnes. Snatch blocks could be used to increase this capacity to 100 tonnes. The winch was normally used at the front, with the bulldozer blade to anchor the vehicle, but it could also be used to the rear for self-recovery.

The bulldozer blade was 3.1m wide and hydraulically driven, using controls at the driver's station. A BREM-1 could use this blade to create an MBT firing position in 12 to 20 minutes, depending on the state of the soil.

For towing, the vehicle had a pair of 1.68m towing rods, with internal shock absorbers, and a pair of 5.5m tow lines. Loads of up to 50 tonnes could be towed for prolonged periods, at the cost of greatly increased fuel consumption.

Other equipment included a 30-tonne capacity hydraulic jack, R-123U radio, tank telephone system, navigation system, and NBC protection. Armour protection was the same as the T-72 MBT, although the only armament was a 12.7mm NSVT machine gun with 840 rounds of ammunition. Four smoke-grenade dischargers were sometimes fitted, and all vehicles could create a smokescreen by injecting diesel fuel into the exhaust manifold.

SPECIFICATIONS: BREM-1

Crew: 3
Weight: 41 tonnes
Length: 7.98m
Width: 3.46m
Height: 2.43m
Ground clearance: 0.46m
Maximum road speed: 60km/hour
Maximum road range: 700km
Gradient: 60%
Vertical obstacle: 0.85m
Armament: 1x 12.7mm NSVT MG (840 rounds)

BREM-2

The BREM-2 was an ARV based on the BMP-1 IFV. The turret was removed and replaced by an armoured plate. A swivelling jib crane was fitted on the hull roof, with a 1.5-tonne capacity (sufficient to lift a BMP power unit). A stowage platform with a capacity of 1.5 tonnes was fitted to the rear of the roof. A variety of recovery equipment, including a welding kit, was stowed around the hull roof and sides.

BREM-2

The interior was rearranged to carry a four-man crew, 6.5 tonne winch, and five folding seats for passengers. It had an NBC protection system, six smoke-grenade launchers, and a 7.62mm PKT machine gun.

Specifications: BREM-2

Crew: 4+5
Weight: 14 tonnes
Length: 7.68m
Width: 3.16m
Height: 2.27m
Maximum road speed: 65km/hour
Maximum road range: 550km
Armament: 1x 7.62mm PKT MG (1,000 rounds)

BREhM-D

The BREhM-D was an ARV based on the chassis of the BTR-D airborne armoured personnel carrier. Specialised equipment included a hydraulic crane, recovery winch, and bulldozer blade (which doubled as a spade to stabilise the vehicle). Towing equipment and a welding kit were also carried.

The crane boom was stowed in a frame on the upper hull when not in use. This crane had a traverse of 150° and reach of 2m. Lift capacity was at least 1.5 tonnes, depending on the number of cable runs used. Cable runs were rigged to the top of the hull. The crane was operated from the commander's position, using power from the vehicle hydraulic system. A hand pump could be used when the engine was not running.

The hydraulic winch had a capacity of 3.5 tonnes, using the main cable. Additional cable runs could be used to increase this to 10.5 tonnes. Like the crane, the winch was controlled from the commander's station. When performing heavy recovery tasks, the bulldozer blade would be manually lowered and used as an anchoring spade. The winch cable was 100m long, and fed through heavy rubber rollers that kept it free of mud and snow.

A pair of telescopic tow bars, fitted with shock absorbers, were carried on the rear of the hull. Folding seats were provided for up to four passengers. A 7.62mm PKT machine gun was fitted in the bow, and the vehicle had smoke-grenade dischargers and NBC protection.

Specifications: BREhM-D

Crew: 3+4
Weight: 8 tonnes
Length: 5.89m

Width: 2.63m
Height: 1.82m
Maximum road speed: 61km/hour
Maximum road range: 500km
Gradient: 60%
Armament: 1x 7.62mm PKT MG (1,000 rounds)

BTR-50PK(B)

Since many light armoured vehicles in the Warsaw Pact armies were amphibious, there was a requirement for an amphibious recovery vehicle. The BTR-50PK(B) was developed to fulfil this need. Like the original BTR-50P upon which it was based, it was fully amphibious, and propelled in the water by a pair of water jets. These provided enough power to tow an amphibious AFV through the water.

Recovery equipment included tow couplings at the rear, towing cables, and quick-release and standard shackles. Because of its amphibious recovery role, it carried life belts and life jackets. A set of RG-UF life-saving equipment was carried, but only for use in emergency, and only if no properly qualified divers were available. The crew consisted of commander and driver, although there was provision for up to four other personnel. Up to eight rescued personnel could be accommodated during recovery operations.

MTP-1 (Bulgaria)

This was a variant of the MT-LBus (often referred to as the ACRV in the West), which was built in Bulgaria under licence. It was used for recovering damaged vehicles, changing components, and preparing positions. Virtually identical to the MT-LBus, it had the same turret as the standard MT-LB, although some

MTP-1

mounted a 12.7mm machine gun in place of the standard 7.62mm PKT.

A crane was mounted in a small turret on the roof, providing the operator with all-round armour protection. The crane extended to 5m, with a capacity of 2 tonnes when fully extended, rising to 3 tonnes when extended no further than 3.4m.

An entrenching blade was mounted at the rear of the vehicle on hydraulic arms, and could prepare a position for a vehicle in around two hours. A rear-mounted winch had a capacity of 30 tonnes when the blade was used to anchor the vehicle, or 10 tonnes with the blade raised.

The MTP-1 had NBC protection and was fully amphibious, propelled in the water by its tracks.

AD-090 Wheeled Recovery Vehicle (Czechoslovakia)

The AD-090 was based on a Tatra 138 6x6 lorry chassis, with a rear-mounted hydraulically-operated 9-tonne capacity crane, and 8-tonne capacity winch. It was normally used in conjunction with a 10-tonne capacity towing axle.

SPECIFICATIONS: AD-090

Weight: 15.9 tonnes
Length: 9.25m
Width: 2.45m
Height: 3.08m (travelling)
Maximum road speed: 60km/hour

VT-34 (CZECHOSLOVAKIA)

The Czech army developed a T-34-based ARV, designated VT-34, borrowing heavily from concepts found in the wartime German Bergepanther. It had a box-shaped superstructure at the rear, a winch, and an entrenching spade that could be used to anchor the vehicle. The VT-34 saw service with the Czech and Polish armies.

VT-34

VT-55A (CZECHOSLOVAKIA)

The VT-55A was a Czech armoured recovery vehicle based on a T-55 hull. A hydraulic crane was fitted on the right of the hull, with a capacity of 1.5 tonnes. The rear of the hull roof held a 2m

VT-55A

x 1.6m platform, which could carry loads of up to 3 tonnes. Two winches were fitted. The primary winch was driven mechanically by the vehicle's engine, and had a capacity of 44 tonnes. The secondary winch was hydraulically operated, with a capacity of 800kg.

Several tow bars and a 4.2m tow cable were carried. Welding equipment, a workbench, and a vice were fitted above one of the tracks, and could be pulled out for use. A spade was fitted at the rear, and could also be used as a bulldozer blade. Fittings for mine-clearing rollers were mounted at the front.

A 7.62mm machine gun was fitted in a small turret, with 360° traverse and sufficient elevation for use against aerial targets. The vehicle had a crew of four, NBC protection, infra-red night-vision equipment, and a snorkel for deep wading.

Specifications: VT-55A

Crew: 3.14
Weight: 36.5 tonnes
Length: 8.3m
Width: 3.4m
Height: 2.52m
Ground clearance: 0.43m
Maximum road speed: 50km/hour
Maximum road range: 270km
Gradient: 32%
Armament: 1x 7.62mm MG

VT-72B (Czechoslovakia)

The VT-72B was developed by Czechoslovakia. Like the Soviet BREM-1, it was based on a T-72 chassis, but differed in several ways from the Soviet vehicle. It was intended to tow stricken vehicles to a safe place, where repairs could be effected. It had a crew of two (driver and commander), although an extra three could be accommodated in the armoured superstructure.

The main recovery winch was hydrostatic, with 200m of cable and a traction force of 300kN when used with the provided pulley system. A secondary 10kN winch had 400m of cable. A front bulldozer blade could be used as an anchor when recovering heavy loads. The blade could also clear obstacles and debris or create emplacements for vehicles.

A hydraulic crane was fitted on the right front of the hull, on a small turntable with full 360° traverse. The crane had a lift capacity of 19 tonnes and a reach of 7.6m. A platform at the rear of the vehicle, measuring 1.4m x 1.4m, could carry loads of up to

4 tonnes. Tools and welding equipment were included for carrying out repairs to recovered vehicles.

A 12.7mm NSV machine gun was fitted, primarily for air defence. Extra fuel could be carried in drums or jerry cans, fitted on racks at the rear.

VPV (Czechoslovakia)

The VPV was an armoured recovery vehicle based on a Czech-built BMP chassis, and was similar to the Soviet BREM-2. The turret was replaced with a cable drum, and a traversable 5-tonne crane was fitted at the rear of the hull roof. The crane could extend to a maximum length of 4.5m. A winch was fitted, which had a tractive force of 125kN, though this could be increased by the use of pulleys. A hydraulically-operated spade was fitted to anchor the vehicle when the winch was in use. A welding set and cutting devices were carried, and both crew members would be trained welders. Like the BMP, the VPV was fully amphibious, propelled in the water by its tracks.

SU-76 Armoured Workshop Vehicle (DDR)

This was a Soviet SU-76, extensively modified to meet the East German army's requirement for a fully-tracked armoured repair vehicle. The gun and ammunition racks were removed, overhead armour added, and a stowage area added between the driver and superstructure.

The driver is seated in the front centre, with the working area at the rear, with a single door for access. The engine is to the right of the driver, with the fuel and batteries to his left. In place of the original two engines were replaced with a single engine of East German design. Equipment included a bench, drill press, generator, lathe, small forge, vice and welding kit. There was no winch for recovery operations, but it was used for repairing components.

Specifications: SU-76 Armoured Workshop Vehicle

Crew: 4
Weight: 11.2 tonnes
Length: 5m (travelling)
Width: 2.74m (travelling)
Height: 2.1m (travelling)
Ground clearance: 0.3m
Maximum road speed: 45km/hour
Maximum road range: 360km
Gradient: 47%
Vertical obstacle: 0.65m

Armour:
Glacis plate: 25mm @ 30° [Effective: 29mm]
Superstructure front: 25mm @ 27° [Effective: 28mm]
Superstructure sides: 12mm @ 17° [Effective: 13mm]
Hull sides: 16mm
Hull top: 10mm
Rear: 15mm
Belly: 10mm

WPT-TOPAS (Poland)

This Polish vehicle was based on the Czech OT-62A APC, which itself was similar to the Soviet BTR-50. In Polish service, the WPT-TOPAS was designated a "technical support vehicle". The East German army also used it, designating it a "recovery, maintenance, and repair vehicle".

The hull was of welded steel armour, with a crew compartment at the front. The engine and transmission were to the rear. The driver was sat at the front centre, with a semi-circular bay to either side of him, and the commander in the bay his left. The bay to his right had an armoured mounting for a 7.62mm machine gun, with full 360° traverse.

The vehicle was fully amphibious, propelled in the water by a pair of water jets at up to 10.8km/hour. Before entering the water, a trim board was erected and bilge pumps switched on. It also had an NBC protection system and infra-red night-vision equipment.

Engineering equipment included a 2.5-tonne winch with 600m of cable and a 1-tonne capacity hand-operated crane that could be mounted at various points. Spare parts, welding equipment, tools, and a four-man tent were also carried.

Specifications: WPT-TOPAS

Crew: 5
Weight: 15 tonnes
Length: 7m
Width: 3.14m
Height: 2.72m
Ground clearance: 0.41m
Maximum road speed: 60km/hour
Maximum road range: 500km
Gradient: 55%
Vertical obstacle: 1.1m
Armament: 1x 7.62mm PK MG

ARMOUR:
Hull front: 11mm
Hull sides: 14mm
Hull top: 10mm
Hull rear: 10mm
Belly: 10mm

WZT-1 (POLAND)

In the late 1960s, Poland started work on its own ARV, the WZT-1. Production started in 1970, using a T-54 chassis, and based on the Soviet T-54-T. It had a 25-tonne powered winch, with pulleys to increase the capacity to 50 tonnes. An auxiliary winch, towing equipment, and 1.5-tonne capacity crane were also fitted. A large spade was provided, which could anchor the vehicle when the winch was in use. It had night-vision equipment, NBC protection for the crew, and could produce smoke by injecting diesel into the exhaust. A 12.7mm DShK heavy machine gun was carried.

WZT-2 (POLAND)

The WZT-2 was similar to the earlier WZT-1, but based on the T-55 chassis. In service in the Polish army from 1973, it was also supplied to India, Iraq, and Yugoslavia. It had a hydraulically operated crane, winch, bulldozer blade, and welding equipment. The bulldozer blade could be used to prepare fighting positions. The vehicle could also be used as an emergency ambulance, able to carry up to three stretcher cases. Other equipment included a deep-wading snorkel and NBC protection, and it could create smoke by injecting diesel into the exhaust. A 12.7mm DShK heavy machine gun was fitted for local defence.

WZT-3 (POLAND)

With the introduction of the T-72 tank, a new ARV was required, and the obvious design decision for the Poles was to base it on Polish-made T-72M hulls. Tests and trials were carried out from 1986 to 1988, following which it was accepted into service with the Polish army.

Up to four crew could be carried, although only the driver and commander were required. Both sat at the front, the driver on the left, with the commander to his right. Both had night-vision devices, and the commander had a cupola mounting a 12.7mm NSV machine gun. A crew hatch was fitted in the centre of the superstructure roof, with a load-carrying platform to the rear. This platform measured 1.91m x 2.16m, with 0.62m-high sides, and had a load capacity of 3.5 tonnes.

A bulldozer blade was fitted at the front, which could be used for anchoring the vehicle as well as excavating. A TD-50 crane was fitted on a small turntable at the front left of the superstructure. This had a lift capacity of 15 tonnes, a reach of 5.8m, and a maximum hook height of 8.6m. The main winch was mechanical, with a pulling capacity of 840kN with tackle, and 200m of cable. A secondary hydraulic winch was also provided. This had a pulling capacity of 20kN, and 400m of cable.

A snorkel allowed the vehicle to wade through water obstacles at a depth of up to 5m, and extra fuel drums could be fitted to the rear.

WZT-3

SPECIFICATIONS: WZT-3

Crew: up to 4
Weight: 42 tonnes
Length: 8.3m
Width: 3.6m
Height: 2.17m
Ground clearance: 0.43m
Maximum road speed: 60km/hour
Maximum road range: 650km
Vertical obstacle: 0.7m
Armament: 1x 12.7mm NSV MG

Earth-Moving Equipment

The Warsaw Pact armies placed a good deal of emphasis on digging shelters. As with other areas, speed was important. Specialised machines were developed to excavate and dig earth far faster than could be achieved with manpower.

As well as the specialised vehicles described in this section, fittings for entrenching blades were mounted on the bow of T-54 and T-55 tanks. The bulldozer blades were designated BTU and BTU-55, and either blade could be fitted to either model of tank. The later BTU-55 was lighter (1.4 tonnes rather than the BTU's 2.3 tonnes), had better performance, and could be fitted and removed more quickly. The T-64, T-72, and T-80 tanks had entrenching blades fitted as standard, which were stowed under the front lower hull when not in use.

BAT Digger

The BAT (also referred to as the BAT-1) was based on the AT-T artillery tractor. It had a large bulldozer blade at the front, which was lifted above the vehicle when in transit. A 20-tonne winch was also fitted. The original version used an electro-pneumatic system to lift the bulldozer blade, while the later BAT-M lifted the blade hydraulically. The BAT-M also added a 2-tonne capacity jib crane with 360° traverse and 70° elevation.

BAT-M

The BAT's primary roles were the speedy construction of roads, approaches to bridges and crossing sites, and filling in obstructions such as ditches. It was also used for felling trees, removing stumps and boulders, and digging emplacements. Attachments were available to convert the basic demolition blade to a V-blade, bulldozer, or angle dozer.

SPECIFICATIONS: BAT

Weight: 25.3 tonnes
Length: 10m
Width: 4.78m
Height: 2.95m
Maximum road speed: 35km/hour
Maximum road range: 700km
Vertical obstacle: 1m
Working speed: 1.5-10km/hour

Specifications: BAT-M

Weight: 27.5 tonnes
Length: 7m (travelling)
Width: 4.85m
Maximum road speed: 35km/hour
Maximum road range: 550km
Vertical obstacle: 1m
Working speed: 1.5-10km/hour

BAT-2 Digger

The BAT-2 was based on the MT-T tracked carrier chassis, which in turn used suspension and running gear components from the T-64 tank. It had the same bulldozer blade as the earlier BAT-M, but the hydraulic system was more powerful. A different system was used to raise the blade vertically when it was not in use.

An armoured cab at the front could carry the crew of two, and there was a compartment to the rear for an eight-man combat engineer squad. There was space for combat engineering stores behind the cab.

A crane was mounted on top of the vehicle. This had a lift capacity of 2 tonnes and a boom outreach of 7.3m. Alongside the crane was a 25-tonne capacity winch with 100m of cable.

The BAT-2 could create graded tracks over normal terrain at a rate of 6.8km/hour, and at up to 8.15km/hour in snow. Terrain with trees of up to 300mm diameter could be cleared at a rate of 2.3km/hour. The bulldozer blade had a clearing capacity of 350-450m3/hour when route-clearing or creating earth barriers, 200-250m3/hour when digging ditches. Solid or frozen ground could be loosened down to a depth of 500mm.

SPECIFICATIONS: BAT-2

Crew: 2+8
Weight: 39.7 tonnes
Length: 9.64m (travelling)
Width: 4.2m
Height: 3.69m
Ground clearance: 0.43m
Maximum road speed: 60km/hour
Maximum road range: 500km

BTM and BTM-TMG Digger and Ditcher

These vehicles were based on the AT-T artillery tractor chassis. The BTM was introduced in 1958, and had a civilian bucket excavator. This mounted 10 to 12 buckets on a rotary frame, which was lifted onto the rear of the vehicle for transit. Before use, it was lowered to the ground at the rear of the vehicle. The BTM-TMG, introduced in 1968, had reinforced buckets to allow operation in frozen ground. This version normally mounted 8 to 10 buckets on the frame.

SPECIFICATIONS: BTM

Crew: 2
Weight: 26.5 tonnes
Length: 7.35m (travelling)
Width: 3.2m
Height: 4.3m (travelling)
Maximum road speed: 35km/hour
Maximum road range: 500km

BTM

Specifications: BTM-TMG

Crew: 2
Weight: 30 tonnes
Length: 7.6m (travelling)
Width: 3.2m
Height: 4.3m (travelling)
Maximum road speed: 36km/hour
Maximum road range: 400km

PZM AND PZM-2 DIGGER AND DITCHER

The PZM was based on the T-150K four-wheel tractor, while the PZM-2 was based on the newer T-155 tractor. Both had a front-mounted bulldozer blade. These vehicles mounted buckets in an arrangement akin to a conveyor belt, driven from the main engine. The transmission had to be disconnected when the excavator was in use. A front-mounted hydro-mechanical winch

PZM-2

was used to pull the vehicle forward when digging. The digger was raised and lowered manually.

SPECIFICATIONS: PZM

Crew: 2
Weight: 13.2 tonnes
Length: 7m (travelling)
Width: 2.52m
Height: 3.75m (travelling)
Maximum road speed: 45km/hour
Maximum road range: 500km

MDK-2 AND MDK-3 EXCAVATOR

The MDK-2, introduced in 1965, was based on an AT-T artillery tractor chassis. It mounted a large rotary digger at the

MDK-2

rear to excavate earth, and a hydraulically-operated bulldozer blade at the front. When in transit, the digger was mounted horizontally behind the cab. It was swung around to a vertical position at the rear of the vehicle for operation. The improved MDK-2M was largely similar, but had a faster working speed. The later MDK-3 was based on the MT-T tractor chassis, with an armoured cab. The MDK series were used to dig trenches, vehicle positions, and gun pits.

SPECIFICATIONS: MDK-2 (MDK-2M IN BRACKETS)

Crew: 2
Weight: 27 tonnes (28 tonnes)
Length: 8m (travelling)
Width: 4m (travelling) (3.4m)
Height: 3.95m (travelling)

Maximum road speed: 35km/hour

Vertical obstacle: 1m (0.65m)

SPECIFICATIONS: MDK-3

Crew: 2

Weight: 40 tonnes

Length: 10m (travelling)

Width: 3.2m (travelling)

Height: 4m (travelling)

Maximum road speed: 50km/hour

Maximum road range: 500km

E-305V SINGLE-BUCKET CRANE SHOVEL

Mounted on a KrAZ-214 6x6 7-tonne lorry, this could be used for digging, or as a crane. The shovel had a capacity of 0.3m3 and could dig 50 to 60m3 per hour. As a crane, it had a lift capacity of 5 tonnes.

DOK BULLDOZER (CZECHOSLOVAKIA)

The DOK fitted a bulldozer blade at the front of a four-wheeled, articulated chassis, with a rear-mounted engine. An electric winch was fitted to the rear of the cab. A multi-purpose bucket was normally fitted, although a snowplough was also available. The cab was hermetically sealed with a filtered ventilation system, providing NBC protection for the operator.

There were three variants: the DOK-L had a universal shovel; the DOK-R had a V-shaped blade that could form a straight blade. The DOK-M was a variant of the DOK-L, with a saw tooth edge and central ridge added to the shovel. The DOK-M also had hydraulic steering, improved brakes, and improved hydraulics.

The DOK saw service in the Czech and East German armies.

SPECIFICATIONS: DOK

Crew: 1
Weight: 28 tonnes
Length: 10.53m (travelling)
Width: 3.15m (travelling)
Height: 3.15m (travelling)
Ground clearance: 0.45m
Maximum road speed: 50km/hour
Maximum cross-country range: 250km
Towed load: 65 tonnes

Image Credits

River Crossing

MTU-20: Vitaly Kuzmin (Creative Commons Attribution-Share Alike 4.0 International)

MT-55A: Srđan Popović (Creative Commons Attribution-Share Alike 4.0 International)

MTU-72: Vitaly Kuzmin (Creative Commons Attribution-Share Alike 4.0 International)

TMM-3: David Holt (Creative Commons Attribution-Share Alike 2.0 Generic)

PMP pontoon: Bin im Garten (Creative Commons Attribution-Share Alike 3.0 Unported)

GSP vehicle unit: (Creative Commons Attribution-Share Alike 3.0 Unported)

PTS-M: Gwafton (Creative Commons Attribution-Share Alike 3.0 Unported)

PTS-2: Vitaly Kuzmin (Creative Commons Attribution-Share Alike 4.0 International)

BMK-T: ShinePhantom (Creative Commons Attribution-Share Alike 3.0 Unported)

KH-200: Kerim44 (Creative Commons Attribution-Share Alike 3.0 Unported)

NZhM-56: Vitaly Kuzmin (Creative Commons Attribution-Share Alike 4.0 International)

Mine Warfare

GMZ-2: Vitaly Kuzmin (Creative Commons Attribution-Share Alike 4.0 International)
GMZ-3: Vitaly Kuzmin (Creative Commons Attribution-Share Alike 4.0 International)
PMR-3: Mike1979 Russia (Creative Commons Attribution-Share Alike 4.0 International)
IMP mine detector: Johan Fredriksson (Creative Commons Attribution-Share Alike 3.0 Unported)

Armoured Engineer Vehicles

IRM: Vitaly Kuzmin (Creative Commons Attribution-Share Alike 4.0 International)

Armoured Recovery Vehicles

VT-34: Vikiped at Russian Wikipedia (Creative Commons Attribution-Share Alike 3.0 Unported)
BREM-1: Vitaly Kuzmin (Creative Commons Attribution-Share Alike 4.0 International)
BREM-2: Vitaly Kuzmin (Creative Commons Attribution-Share Alike 4.0 International)
MTP-1: Scott at Flickr (Creative Commons Attribution-Share Alike 2.0 Generic)
WZT-3: Pibwl (Creative Commons Attribution-Share Alike 3.0 Unported)

Earth-Moving Equipment

BAT-M: Vitaly Kuzmin (CC-BY-SA 4.0 International)

BTM: Vitaly Kuzmin (CC-BY-SA 4.0 International)
PZM-2: User:Cooper6 (CC-BY-SA 3.0 Unported)

Digital Reinforcements: Free Ebook

To get a free ebook of this title, simply scan the code below, or go to www.shilka.co.uk/dr and enter code WPCE64.

The free ebook can be downloaded in several formats: Mobi (for Kindle devices & apps), ePub (for other ereaders & ereader apps), and PDF (for reading on a computer). Ereader apps are available for all computers, tablets and smartphones.

About Russell Phillips

Russell Phillips writes books and articles about military technology and history. His articles have been published in Miniature Wargames, Wargames Illustrated, and the Society of Twentieth Century Wargamers' Journal. Some of these articles are available on his website. He has been interviewed on BBC Radio Stoke and The Voice of Russia.

To get a free book and advance notice of new books, join Russell's mailing list at www.rpbook.co.uk/freebook. You can unsubscribe at any time.

For a full listing of Russell's books, go to www.rpbook.co.uk/books.

Find Russell Phillips Online

Website: www.rpbook.co.uk
Twitter: @RPBook
Facebook: RussellPhillipsBooks
Goodreads: RussellPhillips
E-mail: russell@rpbook.co.uk
Join Russell's mailing list at: www.rpbook.co.uk/freebook

Index

Introduction 1
River Crossing 3
    Snorkelling 4
    Swimming 6
    Vehicle-Launched Bridges 7
        MTU-54 8
        MT-34 (Czechoslovakia) 9
        MTU-20 10
        BLG-60 (Poland/DDR) 12
        MT-55A (Czechoslovakia) 13
        MTU-72 15
        KMM 17
        TMM 18
        AM-50 (Czechoslovakia) 20
        SMT-1 (Poland) 20
    Pontoon Bridges 22
        LPP 22
        TMP 23
        TPP 24
        PMP 24
        PVD-20 26
        TZI 27
        PPS 27
        DPP-40 27
        LPB (DDR) 28
        PP-64 (Poland) 29
        LMS (Czechoslovakia) 30

SMS (Czechoslovakia)...30
PR-60 (Romania)..31
Amphibians and Ferries..32
   K-61...32
   GSP...33
   PTS..35
   PMM-2..36
   PTS-2..36
Bridging Boats..37
   BMK-70 and BMK-90..38
   BMK-130...39
   BMK-150...40
   BMK-T..41
   BB-120 (DDR)...42
   KH-200 (Poland)...43
   Mo-108, Mo-111, Mo-930 (Czechoslovakia)..............44
Line of Communication Bridges..................................45
   PVM, LVM, TVM Suspension Bridges.....................46
   MARM...47
   SARM..47
   BARM...47
   NZhM-56..48
   RMM-4...49
   REM-500..49
   SP-19 Self-Propelled Pontoon Bridge......................50
   TMS (Czechoslovakia)..50
   MS-1 (Czechoslovakia)...50
   DMS-65 (Poland)..51
   ESB-16 (DDR)..51

SBG-66 (DDR) 51
SB-30 and SB-45 (DDR) 52
Mine Warfare 53
   Minelaying 53
      Helicopter Minelaying Equipment 54
      GMZ and GMZ-2 54
      GMZ-3 56
      PMR-2, PMR-3, and PMZ-4 57
      UMZ 59
      MLG-60 (DDR) 59
   Mine Detection 60
      VIM-625 and VIM-695 Portable Mine Detectors 60
      VIM-203M Metallic Mine Detector 61
      UMIV-1 Portable Mine Detector 61
      IMP Portable Mine Detector 61
      DIM Vehicle-Mounted Mine Detector 62
      VISF Model 1946 Portable Mine Detector (Bulgaria)
      63
      M62 Portable Mine Detector (Bulgaria) 63
      M-10 and M-11 Portable Mine Detectors
      (Czechoslovakia) 64
      MSG 64 Portable Mine Detector (DDR) 64
   Mine Clearance 64
      PT-54, PT-54M, and PT-55 Mine Rollers 65
      KMT-4 Mine Plough 66
      KMT-5 Mine Plough and Rollers 67
      KMT-6 Mine Plough 68
      KMT-7 Mine Plough and Rollers 68
      KMT-8 Mine Plough 68

KMT-10 Mine Plough..69
MTK Armoured Mine-Clearing Vehicle......................70
MTK-2 Armoured Mine-Clearing Vehicle.................70
ITB-2, SPZ-2, and SPZ-4..71
BDT..71
UZ-1 and UZ-2 Bangalore Torpedoes........................72
PW-LWD (Poland)...72
Tank-Mounted Rollers and Ploughs (Czechoslovakia)
....73
Trailer-based system (Czechoslovakia).......................74
Armoured Engineer Vehicles..75
IMR Combat Engineer Vehicle....................................75
IMR-2 Combat Engineer Vehicle................................76
IRM Engineer Reconnaissance Vehicle.......................77
ADZM Engineer Vehicle...80
MT-LB Engineer Vehicles..80
Recovery and Repair Vehicles..83
T-34 ARVs..83
IS-T..84
BTS-1..84
BTS-2..84
BTS-3..85
T-54 (A) and T-54 (B) (DDR).......................................85
BREM-64..85
BREM-1..86
BREM-2..88
BREhM-D...90
BTR-50PK(B)...91
MTP-1 (Bulgaria)...91

AD-090 Wheeled Recovery Vehicle (Czechoslovakia) 92
VT-34 (Czechoslovakia)..................................93
VT-55A (Czechoslovakia)................................93
VT-72B (Czechoslovakia)................................95
VPV (Czechoslovakia).....................................96
SU-76 Armoured Workshop Vehicle (DDR)..............96
WPT-TOPAS (Poland)....................................97
WZT-1 (Poland)...99
WZT-2 (Poland)...99
WZT-3 (Poland)...100
Earth-Moving Equipment..................................103
BAT Digger..103
BAT-2 Digger...105
BTM and BTM-TMG Digger and Ditcher..............106
PZM and PZM-2 Digger and Ditcher.....................107
MDK-2 and MDK-3 Excavator............................108
E-305V Single-Bucket Crane Shovel......................110
DOK Bulldozer (Czechoslovakia).........................110
Image Credits..113
River Crossing..113
Mine Warfare...114
Armoured Engineer Vehicles.............................114
Armoured Recovery Vehicles............................114
Earth-Moving Equipment................................114
Digital Reinforcements: Free Ebook......................117
About Russell Phillips.....................................119
Find Russell Phillips Online..............................119

www.ingramcontent.com/pod-product-compliance
Lightning Source LLC
Chambersburg PA
CBHW020618300426
44113CB00007B/696